I0575358

25th Anniversary
The Liberation of Kuwait
Honoring the Veterans of Desert Storm

First Edition © 2016 Remember My Service Productions, a division of StoryRock, Inc.
Unless credited otherwise, all photographs and copyrights herein are provided by
U.S. National Archives and Records Administration (NARA).

All rights reserved. No part of this book may be reproduced or
distributed in any form by any means without permission from the publisher,
Remember My Service Productions.

RememberMyService.com

For more information about this book, please visit:
LiberationOfKuwait.com

Library of Congress Cataloging-in-Publication Data

25th Anniversary
The Liberation of Kuwait
Honoring the Veterans of Desert Storm

ISBN: 978-0-9863285-1-0

I am very pleased to join in this important project honoring the courage of an unprecedented coalition force, along with the shared commitment to principle and collective determination that liberated Kuwait 25 years ago.

Together, we denounced the unlawful and unprovoked aggression by which a brutal dictator attempted to subsume the sovereign nation of Kuwait.

Together, we condemned the savage acts of evil perpetrated against its proud and peaceful people.

Together, we declared that the aggression against Kuwait would not stand.

And together, our service men and women stepped into the breach and ejected the occupying forces in decisive fashion.

Looking back, I am proud that the United States was able to work in concert with our respected allies to help right a historic wrong. It was highly satisfying, too, to see the United Nations working as its founders envisioned—serving not only as a forum for debate and discussion, but noble action as well.

Most of all, it is my hope that in so looking back at this proud chapter in history, we can also look forward with renewed confidence to the future, knowing that such principled action in the face of depravity is not only possible, but required of a civilized world.

— *Hon. George H. W. Bush*
   41st President of the United States of America

On behalf of the State of Kuwait, as the Founding and Supporting Partner, we offer the heartfelt gratitude of the people and government of Kuwait to those Veterans of the Gulf War and Liberators of Kuwait for their service in Operation Desert Storm.

From the beginning of this 25th anniversary commemorative endeavor, we have supported this special project to recognize the service and sacrifice of American and Kuwaiti service men and women, and all those worthy members of the Gulf War Coalition, and honor the memory of those who lost their lives in the war to liberate Kuwait.

Since the liberation, we have rebuilt our nation and continue our tradition of contributing toward the humanitarian relief of other nations.

Thank you.

It is my profound honor to offer every American Veteran of Desert Storm and the Liberation of Kuwait my heartfelt gratitude for your service and sacrifice 25 years ago. This special anniversary to me constitutes the commemoration of not only our liberation, but more so the binding together of two great peoples, an alliance of friendship that goes back a century and more. Because of America's willingness to come to the aid of my country, today the free nation of Kuwait prospers, its people going about their lives able to enjoy their liberties and their comforts without struggling under the oppression of a tyrant. I thank you, all those who served and who suffered to free my people. More so, I honor those who made the ultimate sacrifice.

Following that fateful day of 02 August 1990, as a younger man, I was closely involved with the resistance against tyranny during the occupation. I witnessed the brutalities of Saddam's henchmen, but was inspired by the many individual and heroic sacrifices made by both Kuwaitis, as well as many expatriates. I got to know American and other coalition Soldiers, Sailors, Airmen, and Marines. I saw the efforts made by a host of unsung heroes, many giving their lives so that others might live. However, perhaps the greatest message for me, which the war taught so forcefully, is that freedom is a truly rare, even priceless, gift. It does not grow naturally or sprout from nothing. It never "just happens." It must be bought at a high price, often requiring much pain and sacrifice, and then nurtured and protected by a dedicated few, these values passed from parent to child.

Tragically, too often the next generation forgets what was achieved in its behalf. We as a nation and a people must never allow that to happen. More so, we must try to live our lives so that we are worthy of what you heroes have done for each of us. In the case of Kuwait, we as a nation, and individually, must remember to continue to use our freedoms, which were paid for at great cost, to provide help and assistance to others, especially those less fortunate, or those who are oppressed. We as a nation and a people know how that feels. We also know that by working together with our allies and friends that we can overcome any obstacle placed in our path. These are the lessons of Desert Storm, the lessons we must teach our children.

Again, thank you to my American friends, to all those who served and for setting a strong example of selfless service to the world. And thank you to the families—the spouses, children, and parents—of those who made the ultimate sacrifice. You will always have my highest admiration and respect. Please accept my countrymen's and my sincere and profound thank-you. Twenty five years ago, you gave us back our country.

Sincerely,
— Mr. Fouad M.T. Alghanim

25TH ANNIVERSARY
THE
LIBERATION
OF
KUWAIT
HONORING THE VETERANS
OF DESERT STORM

Saddam's troops entering Kuwait City. *Photo courtesy of Kuwait Ministry of Information.*

Photo courtesy of Kuwait Ministry of Information.

TABLE OF CONTENTS

Many Kuwaitis fell victim to death, torture, and catastrophic injury from the invading forces of Saddam Hussein. *Photo courtesy of Kuwait Ministry of Information.*

A U.S. Army captain holds up a girl waving a Kuwaiti flag as civilians and Coalition military forces celebrate the retreat of Iraqi forces from Kuwait. *Photo courtesy of NARA.*

REJECTION OF A TYRANT

In September 1990, the border between Iraq and Jordan was swamped with thousands of refugees fleeing Saddam's invasion of Kuwait. I was there. The stories I heard from the mouths of the refugees themselves at the border were unbelievable—the horrors, the hardships, the naked brutality.

Wars are always the hardest on the innocent, the old, the women and children. Saddam forced most of those fleeing refugees to depart Kuwait through Baghdad to gain "permission," then on to the Jordanian frontier. Under Saddam's thumb, they would have the privilege of leaving only if granted by the "Maximum Leader." In reality, such required transit papers and the right to leave came at a price—always.

These newly displaced refugees from Kuwait, many who had come originally for jobs, now fled by any form of transport they could beg or buy. Kuwaitis as well as Indians, Filipinos, Sri Lankans, Africans, Egyptians, Indonesians, Nepalese—tens of thousands and more of the poorest of the poor, sick and weakened by a month of Iraqi occupation in Kuwait, and now subjected to even greater abuse at Iraqi checkpoints along the way. Cars were stolen from them at gunpoint, valuables pilfered, women abused, many left afoot to do whatever they could to somehow catch a ride to the border—and freedom. But even that was a grueling 15-hour journey or more beyond Baghdad, through some of the most hostile desert on earth.

We arrived at the Jordanian-Iraqi border coming from Amman that first week of September. Spread before us was a sight we'll never forget: masses of humanity sprawled on the desert, on blankets and coats and robes, anything and sometimes nothing, crowding the Jordanian border outpost, trying to gain admittance. No latrines or bathrooms—the stench was indescribable. Hugging the border, the refugees, parched and hungry, were trying to comfort their crying children. Many had given all they had just to reach the Jordanian frontier, and now they were left to succumb to fatigue or dehydration.

It was just a month after the invasion, and the desert was lethally hot. Temperatures ranged upwards of 115 degrees-plus by day, then dipped down into the frigid zone by night. On the Jordanian side, the Red Crescent (a Middle East version of the Red Cross), had set up a few tents where nurses and doctors did their best to somehow handle the onslaught. We spoke with a doctor. They were treating as many as 50 scorpion stings and viper bites every night. The suffering was unending. Of course, we tried to help, providing food, blankets, and water that we'd brought along, but that was quickly spent. We were overwhelmed.

We stayed a few days on the border, helping all we could until forced to depart. And as we did, we remember cursing the cause of all this human suffering, the Maximum Leader, the butcher of Baghdad, a man who actually considered himself the modern incarnation of Saladin the Great of Muslim and Middle East historical fame. Saddam Hussein even had posters superimposing his face in that iconic, honored role.

In the end, however, Saddam would be rejected even by his own, the usual demise of such self-serving despots. Everything he touched turned to pain and suffering, especially for the poor and the powerless. And though such tyrants claim to be the champions of the masses and the advocates of the poor, they are, in reality, the common man's worst nightmare. The Gulf War was but one more sad example of the Biblical verse: "When the wicked beareth rule, the people mourn." (King James Version, Prov. 29.2)

Richard Robison
Author, *The Liberation of Kuwait*
Remember My Service Productions

Kuwaiti oil well set ablaze by Saddam's forces. *Photo courtesy of Kuwait Ministry of Information.*

Prologue
EYE OF THE STORM

"This will not stand, this aggression against Kuwait."
—President George H. W. Bush, August 5, 1990

From the beginning, President George Herbert Walker Bush understood the true international impact of Saddam's actions: this was not just an invasion by an aggressive neighbor against peaceful Kuwait. A brutal dictator and megalomaniac had determined that he would literally erase from history an entire nation and people. The tiny yet prosperous nation of Kuwait was facing its greatest historical test. The world had entered a new age—"a new world order," as President Bush called it—one where the rule of law and justice was receiving its first challenge.

Any Kuwaiti citizen old enough to remember can tell you precisely where he or she was on August 2, 1990, when the tanks of Saddam Hussein's vaunted Republican Guard rolled in from the north. The treacherous, surprise attack is etched deeply into the memory of anyone over 40 today. As Pearl Harbor forever changed that generation of Americans, so Saddam's invasion signaled the end of an era—both for the world at large and, especially, for the nation and people of Kuwait.

And those who remember the slogan "Free Kuwait!"—spray-painted on the walls of side streets and shouted from the rooftops by brave patriots who were arrested and never heard from again—still feel that burning pride, that patriotic glue that fashioned a nation from many formerly disparate interests and ethnicities. Kuwait is what it is today because it faced such a deadly challenge and prevailed. Such a victory testifies of the resilience of the Kuwaiti people and keeps alive the memory of those untold number of citizens who Saddam's henchmen secretly buried in the deserts between Kuwait City and Baghdad.

The slogan "Free Kuwait" also gives voice to those unnamed heroes who died in courageous street fighting. Patriotic civilian partisans joined the Kuwaiti military and police who tried desperately, though heavily outnumbered, to defend their homeland. The liberation of Kuwait shows how the world came together—led by the United States, the finest military on earth—to restore freedom and justice, thanks to the heroes we honor today. These selfless veterans, from the United States as well as other Coalition countries, gave so much and asked so little in return. A heartfelt thank you to all who served—this commemorative book is dedicated to you. ∎

REJECTION OF A TYRANT

In September 1990, the border between Iraq and Jordan was swamped with thousands of refugees fleeing Saddam's invasion of Kuwait. I was there. The stories I heard from the mouths of the refugees themselves at the border were unbelievable—the horrors, the hardships, the naked brutality.

Wars are always the hardest on the innocent, the old, the women and children. Saddam forced most of those fleeing refugees to depart Kuwait through Baghdad to gain "permission," then on to the Jordanian frontier. Under Saddam's thumb, they would have the privilege of leaving only if granted by the "Maximum Leader." In reality, such required transit papers and the right to leave came at a price—always.

These newly displaced refugees from Kuwait, many who had come originally for jobs, now fled by any form of transport they could beg or buy. Kuwaitis as well as Indians, Filipinos, Sri Lankans, Africans, Egyptians, Indonesians, Nepalese—tens of thousands and more of the poorest of the poor, sick and weakened by a month of Iraqi occupation in Kuwait, and now subjected to even greater abuse at Iraqi checkpoints along the way. Cars were stolen from them at gunpoint, valuables pilfered, women abused, many left afoot to do whatever they could to somehow catch a ride to the border—and freedom. But even that was a grueling 15-hour journey or more beyond Baghdad, through some of the most hostile desert on earth.

We arrived at the Jordanian-Iraqi border coming from Amman that first week of September. Spread before us was a sight we'll never forget: masses of humanity sprawled on the desert, on blankets and coats and robes, anything and sometimes nothing, crowding the Jordanian border outpost, trying to gain admittance. No latrines or bathrooms—the stench was indescribable. Hugging the border, the refugees, parched and hungry, were trying to comfort their crying children. Many had given all they had just to reach the Jordanian frontier, and now they were left to succumb to fatigue or dehydration.

It was just a month after the invasion, and the desert was lethally hot. Temperatures ranged upwards of 115 degrees-plus by day, then dipped down into the frigid zone by night. On the Jordanian side, the Red Crescent (a Middle East version of the Red Cross), had set up a few tents where nurses and doctors did their best to somehow handle the onslaught. We spoke with a doctor. They were treating as many as 50 scorpion stings and viper bites every night. The suffering was unending. Of course, we tried to help, providing food, blankets, and water that we'd brought along, but that was quickly spent. We were overwhelmed.

We stayed a few days on the border, helping all we could until forced to depart. And as we did, we remember cursing the cause of all this human suffering, the Maximum Leader, the butcher of Baghdad, a man who actually considered himself the modern incarnation of Saladin the Great of Muslim and Middle East historical fame. Saddam Hussein even had posters superimposing his face in that iconic, honored role.

In the end, however, Saddam would be rejected even by his own, the usual demise of such self-serving despots. Everything he touched turned to pain and suffering, especially for the poor and the powerless. And though such tyrants claim to be the champions of the masses and the advocates of the poor, they are, in reality, the common man's worst nightmare. The Gulf War was but one more sad example of the Biblical verse: "When the wicked beareth rule, the people mourn." (King James Version, Prov. 29.2)

Richard Robison
Author, *The Liberation of Kuwait*
Remember My Service Productions

Kuwaiti oil well set ablaze by Saddam's forces. *Photo courtesy of Kuwait Ministry of Information.*

Prologue
EYE OF THE STORM

"This will not stand, this aggression against Kuwait."
—President George H. W. Bush, August 5, 1990

From the beginning, President George Herbert Walker Bush understood the true international impact of Saddam's actions: this was not just an invasion by an aggressive neighbor against peaceful Kuwait. A brutal dictator and megalomaniac had determined that he would literally erase from history an entire nation and people. The tiny yet prosperous nation of Kuwait was facing its greatest historical test. The world had entered a new age—"a new world order," as President Bush called it—one where the rule of law and justice was receiving its first challenge.

Any Kuwaiti citizen old enough to remember can tell you precisely where he or she was on August 2, 1990, when the tanks of Saddam Hussein's vaunted Republican Guard rolled in from the north. The treacherous, surprise attack is etched deeply into the memory of anyone over 40 today. As Pearl Harbor forever changed that generation of Americans, so Saddam's invasion signaled the end of an era—both for the world at large and, especially, for the nation and people of Kuwait.

And those who remember the slogan "Free Kuwait!"—spray-painted on the walls of side streets and shouted from the rooftops by brave patriots who were arrested and never heard from again—still feel that burning pride, that patriotic glue that fashioned a nation from many formerly disparate interests and ethnicities. Kuwait is what it is today because it faced such a deadly challenge and prevailed. Such a victory testifies of the resilience of the Kuwaiti people and keeps alive the memory of those untold number of citizens who Saddam's henchmen secretly buried in the deserts between Kuwait City and Baghdad.

The slogan "Free Kuwait" also gives voice to those unnamed heroes who died in courageous street fighting. Patriotic civilian partisans joined the Kuwaiti military and police who tried desperately, though heavily outnumbered, to defend their homeland. The liberation of Kuwait shows how the world came together—led by the United States, the finest military on earth—to restore freedom and justice, thanks to the heroes we honor today. These selfless veterans, from the United States as well as other Coalition countries, gave so much and asked so little in return. A heartfelt thank you to all who served—this commemorative book is dedicated to you. ■

A U.S. Army captain holds up a girl waving a Kuwaiti flag as civilians and Coalition military forces celebrate the retreat of Iraqi forces from Kuwait. *Photo courtesy of NARA.*

Chapter 1
THE FORGOTTEN WAR

Many Americans and even some younger Kuwaitis view the liberation of Kuwait as another forgotten war in the distant past, much like the Korean War fought decades ago.

A quarter century has passed since February 26, 1991. A new generation has risen. The average age in Kuwait hovers at around 25, and more than a quarter of the population is under 14. This means that most Kuwaitis today have no memory of the Iraqi invasion. Sadly, so many of the heroes of Desert Shield and Desert Storm are no longer with us—like General "Stormin' Norman" Schwarzkopf, who led not only U.S. troops but the entire international coalition of 35 nations against Iraq. General Schwarzkopf passed away December 27, 2012; each year we lose a few more of our honored Gulf War veterans. The potential loss of such critical institutional memory—the stories of bravery and sacrifice and experiences that affected the lives of millions—should trouble all who value history.

This is the hope and purpose behind this commemorative book and its companion feature documentary: that we remember what happened 25 years ago. This great conflict to free a nation and restore a people serves as a stark reminder to the world that the safety and protection of all people everywhere is a responsibility we all share. And a nation's responsibility to those who served, and to the story of our honored veterans, is to never forget.

Those who forget the past are destined to repeat it. Our responsibility and our charge is to remember the forgotten war in Kuwait, and to retell the stories of the service and courage of our veterans. In memory of the Gulf War, we venerate those who served and who made the ultimate sacrifice, not only to free Kuwait and return it to its rightful citizens, but to stand proudly with the nations of the earth in opposition to tyranny. In the case of Kuwait's liberation, this is not just a story that people tell, but the history our honored veterans actually lived.

THE EYE OF THE STORM

Every Kuwaiti understands that the country is situated in a pretty rough neighborhood. Larger, more powerful nations surround Kuwait on every border. To the north stands Iraq. East, across the Gulf of Arabia, stands the Islamic Republic of Iran. South and west, of course, is Kuwait's longtime ally, Saudi Arabia.

In many ways, Kuwait is situated squarely in the eye of the storm—literally and figuratively. The *khamsin* winds that roll off the Iranian highlands and Iraq produce dust storms that blind and disorient and are impossible to describe unless you've experienced one. Similarly, some of the nations that surround Kuwait are struggling with their own political challenges. Still, throughout its history, Kuwait has stood as the clear and calm voice amid conflict and upheaval. Kuwait is indeed the "eye of the storm"—the ever-calming, stable voice calling for civility and reason amid the tumult.

Today, this small country has become a model for many other smaller or less powerful nations the world over, providing a fine example of the power of diplomacy. Even when under attack by Saddam's forces, Kuwait showed the rest of the world how to successfully reach out and garner support from a broad coalition of friends. Led by the determined and capable Bush Administration, global opposition to Saddam's grab of Kuwait grew steadily as the Coalition

President George H. W. Bush peers out from a bunker at an M2 .50 caliber machine gun. The president was visiting U.S. troops deployed to the area during Operation Desert Shield. *Photo courtesy of NARA.*

Kuwaiti student Jasem Al-Habib volunteered for the U.S. Army during the Gulf War. *Photo courtesy of Kuwait Ministry of Information.*

Embedded with U.S. Ground Forces

Jasem Al-Habib was a young Kuwaiti university student in the United States at the time of the invasion in 1990. "I was going to school at the time," he recalls, "and it was so difficult to even attend classes, knowing that your country is being invaded and your family is there and you don't know what is going on there. You don't have any news out of the country."

But soon Al-Habib knew what he must do: find a way to turn his anxiety into action. "When I heard the Kuwaiti Embassy was asking Kuwaiti students if any of us wanted to join the U.S. Army, I thought, what an opportunity! Liberate my own country while serving with the finest military in the world!"

Al-Habib became a volunteer in the U.S. Army, an experience he will always remember. "Anyone who saw what Saddam Hussein did to my people and our country of Kuwait—making thousands disappear, setting fire to hundreds of oil wells, and creating one of the most devastating ecological disasters of modern times—will never forget."

Al-Habib pleads with this new generation of Kuwaitis and Americans to always remember the atrocities of a malevolent dictator. "We need to be sure that people don't take things for granted," he says. "Saddam Hussein did some bad stuff. That's the truth. It's raw. You can't forget that. I haven't."

formed and strengthened. This is the story of one of the most incredible diplomatic and military successes in history.

KUWAIT AND AMERICA—HISTORY INTERTWINED

Americans have a place in Kuwait's history—much more than most people realize. In 1912, the then Amir of Kuwait, Sheikh Mubarak Al-Sabah, invited American Christian missionaries near Baghdad to come to Kuwait and establish a hospital. Christian doctors and nurses representing the American Reformed Church willingly accepted. The result of that provident invitation was the Amricani Hospital, which treated many

Four Principles

"Four simple principles guide our policy. First, we seek the immediate, unconditional, and complete withdrawal of all Iraqi forces from Kuwait. Second, Kuwait's legitimate government must be restored to replace the puppet regime. And third, my administration, as has been the case with every [U.S.] president since Franklin Roosevelt, is committed to the security and stability of the [Arabian] Gulf. And fourth, I am determined to protect the lives of American citizens abroad."

— **President George H. W. Bush,** *August 8, 1990*

Origin of the Name *Kuwait*

Some claim that the name *Kuwait* originates from the Arabic word *akwat*, the plural of *kout*, which means "small fort (built near water)." Most believe it was named in the 17th century by local rulers in reference not only to the size of Kuwait (which is geographically smaller than New Jersey), but also because of what originally was a migrant, seaside population making a living from the trade routes, both land and sea.

wounded in October 1920, during the Jahra Battle against insurgent tribes trying to invade Kuwait City. Later, during an outbreak of smallpox in Kuwait, the hospital staff saved many who would have otherwise succumbed to the deadly disease. The American hospital was often referred to as "the original gateway to modern medicine in Kuwait." It served the people of Kuwait until the 1960s, when modern facilities replaced the old structures. Today, the Amricani Cultural Center is located close to the seaside near Souq Sharq (East) shopping mall.

A TRADITION OF HOSPITALITY AND OPPORTUNITY

Kuwait has always opened its land to foreigners. Millions have worked in Kuwait, many in high-paying jobs, including tens of thousands of Americans. Kuwait has sought from its founding to provide opportunities for anyone willing to work hard and earn success.

Before oil was discovered in Kuwait, this was a land and people disciplined by circumstance—the country is one of the most arid and hottest continually inhabited spots on our globe. The people of Kuwait became some of the hardiest, most resilient, and creative people on earth. They learned quickly to accommodate a harsh environment, both geographically and geopolitically, developing resilience and skill in dealing with powerful and potentially threatening neighbors. Americans, among many others, admired the Kuwaitis' flexibility and quiet toughness in the face of hardship.

Such contact with other nations was the result of diplomatic exchange, business and cultural interaction and cooperation, and, unfortunately, an unavoidable war.

Desert sands of Kuwait.
*Photo courtesy of Kuwait
Ministry of Information.*

An HH-60H Sea Hawk helicopter from Helicopter Combat Support Special Squadron (HCS-4) of Naval Air Station Norfolk, Virginia, takes off in the sand for a search and rescue mission at the start of Operation Desert Storm. *Photo courtesy of NARA.*

Cost of Fresh Water

Kuwait is one of the few nations on earth that has absolutely no sources of fresh, potable water, though some brackish water can be found in several locations. Considering the blistering temperatures for much of the year, this absence of renewable water resources could be lethal. All drinking water in the country must either be shipped in (as it was in the past) or produced on an industrial scale by mammoth desalinization plants located strategically on the coasts of the Gulf. It is not an exaggeration to say that a liter of water costs more than a liter of gasoline in Kuwait.

Tank sunk in the desert. *Photo courtesy of Jim Janda.*

GOD'S BLESSING: LIFE IN A ROUGH NEIGHBORHOOD

In the 18th and 19th centuries, Kuwait turned its Arabian Gulf shoreline into a prosperous port economy. However, after a number of British coastal blockades in the early 20th century put great hardship on the nation, along with the 1938 discovery of vast oil resources, Kuwait—with the help of international oil exploration companies—transformed itself.

Making full use of this new capital-generating commodity between 1946 and 1982, Kuwait invested in a wide array of national infrastructure projects, bringing to the Kuwaiti people the benefits—and challenges—of rapid modernization and ever-climbing personal wealth. But just as Kuwaitis began to participate in phenomenal growth and development and to establish a strong foothold, harsh economic winds again swept over them with the Kuwait stock market crash of the 1980s.

Undaunted, Kuwait recovered and continued to invest in social services, especially expanding and modernizing its educational, medical, cultural, and commercial facilities and oil operations. It also reached out to the world, providing aid and investment in struggling, underdeveloped regions of Asia and Africa. Kuwait's methodical and well-planned economic growth, however, and its extensive investment in the latest and best technologies, did not go unnoticed—the country would become the prey of the rapacious Saddam Hussein on August 2, 1990.

Sand and Dust

Amazingly, the modernization of 20th century Kuwait required the importation of sand. One would think that a desert country like Kuwait would be the last nation on earth to have a shortage of the stuff. But upon closer inspection, the Arabian Desert is not covered with sand, but rather a very fine, almost talcum powder-like dust that lacks the proper silicates necessary to use in concrete.

So, for modern masonry construction, sand must be shipped from other regions of the earth. Arabian desert dust is so fine, in fact, that several times a year heavy *shamal* (north) or *khamsin* winds pick up this desert powder and carry it several thousand feet into the air, threatening airline traffic and encouraging even hardy Kuwaiti shopkeepers to take a "weather holiday."

Concrete Needs

"When I first got to Kuwait, 95 percent of the food had to be brought in. So you would think with all that food being imported, food would be the biggest and heaviest of all imports. Wrong! It's sand. I thought, This is crazy. The whole country is sand! But the sand in Kuwait is not proper for making architectural concrete, and with their building boom, they needed more concrete than food.

"In fact, in 2003 one of the biggest complaints we had, as we were taking up large berth spaces at the port for bringing in all our equipment, was that there were ships full of sand having to wait off the Gulf. We had all these ships stacked up full of sand that needed to be unloaded so it could be turned into concrete to build homes.

"That's why my Kuwaiti friends tell me, 'The hardest thing you will ever do in your life as a Kuwaiti is to build your own home!'"

— **Colonel (ret) Randy Williams**
MPRI-Kuwait National Guard Development Program Manager

Piles of rubble were left in the wake of Saddam's invading troops. *Photo courtesy of Kuwait Ministry of Information.*

Saddam's invaders devastated Kuwaiti schools. *Photo courtesy of Kuwait Ministry of Information.*

SADDAM HUSSEIN

Saddam Hussein Abd Al-Majid Al-Tikriti, Iraq's despot and resident tyrant, had lusted after Kuwait's wealth for some time, particularly following his costly and devastating war with Iran in the 1980s. When Saddam issued the command to his army to invade, no sooner had he controlled Kuwait, than he shamelessly began trying to justify his illegal act.

At first he attempted to use history to rationalize and defend the invasion, citing historical associations as distant as the Ottoman Empire or as recent as the European remapping of Middle Eastern national boundaries following World War I.

Then the self-proclaimed "Maximum Leader" changed tactics. He announced his status as "The Great Protector," stating that he was only liberating Kuwait and defending it from a "nefarious, shadowy conspiracy"—one that was never identified, of course. In his "magnanimity and generosity," Saddam told everyone he would protect Kuwait and its citizens, allowing Kuwait the blessing of becoming the 19th province or governorate of a greater Iraq.

Of course, from Day One of the invasion, no Kuwaiti supported Saddam's transparent power grab, nor did any legitimate international body. In his hubris, in his outrageous arrogance, Saddam stood alone.

THE TREACHERY OF A MADMAN

The excuses Saddam Hussein offered for the invasion of Kuwait were as random and illogical as the man who made them. Soon he was claiming nonsensically that the invasion of Kuwait was "to oppose an uprising against Kuwait's Amir." He had also earlier accused Kuwait of keeping oil prices too low, then alleged that Kuwait was pumping more than its quota from the oil field shared by Kuwait and Iraq on their mutual border. His excuses pathetically proliferated, conspiracy upon conspiracy, his paranoia multiplying with each passing day.

Of course, none of what he was claiming was accepted by the U.N. Security Council, which imposed economic sanctions and passed a series of resolutions in the fall of 1990, condemning Iraq for the unlawful and unprovoked invasion of a peaceful neighbor.

THE METHODS OF A BRUTAL DICTATOR

The FBI's interrogation of Saddam following his capture in 2003 revealed that the Iran-Iraq War also played a major role in

Saddam's ultimate decision to invade Kuwait.

The Iran-Iraq War (1980–1988) had been so costly that Saddam was desperate to obtain financial resources by any means possible to rebuild his power in Iraq. Prior to the Iran-Iraq War, Iraq had $40 billion (USD) in hard currency reserves, largely from the sale of oil. Following the war, Iraq was $80 billion (USD) in debt.

Not only did Saddam resent having to pay back those loans as he had promised, but his infamous paranoia caused him to blame others for his predicament, one that was plainly his responsibility alone. In fact, Saddam had squandered much of Iraq's reserves on costly weapons programs and a self-aggrandizing mega-plan of national monument construction, which poured billions he didn't have into lavish personal palaces, monstrous statues (usually of himself), and extravagant facilities in many regions of Iraq. All this was done while his people were starving and lacking sufficient medical care.

Saddam reasoned that if a wealthy and prosperous Kuwait were, in fact, no longer a sovereign country but Iraq's 19th province, then not only could his debts with Kuwait be wiped clean, but the wealth of Kuwait would be his alone. Of course, only a madman would have viewed a sovereign, nonthreatening nation as his for the taking. Invasion and occupation became Saddam's ultimate solution for all his problems. He even believed that once he had annexed Kuwait, he would have greater control over the international oil markets and global price—and he would have much more of this rich commodity.

In reality, what Saddam could not steal and hoard, he destroyed. The resulting brutalization, pillage, and plunder of Kuwait would not only cause the destruction of Kuwait's oil wells and facilities, but also the theft of medical and scientific technology, equipment, household furnishings, and personal property. In sum, the country of Kuwait was stripped to the bone. Even the proverbial kitchen sink was carted off by Iraqi plunderers.

THE INVASION—AUGUST 2, 1990

So how did Saddam's surprise invasion play out? Of course, tensions between Kuwait and Iraq had been growing for some time. Despite the deterioration of Saddam Hussein's reputation in the international community and worsening relations with Kuwait, still Kuwait was not on a war footing—not yet. So as not to inflame an already difficult international situation, and perhaps because Kuwait did not yet fully appreciate the dangerously unpredictable Saddam Hussein, Kuwaiti armed forces were ordered to stand down on July 19, 1990.

So a small and effectively hobbled Kuwaiti military found itself confronting combat-hardened units of the Iraqi Republican Guard—with fully detailed armored and

Destruction and ruin caused by Saddam Hussein's invasion of Kuwait. *Photo courtesy of Kuwait Ministry of Information.*

Caution

"There were some who felt right away that military action would be required. My position was, let's examine the alternatives. Let's see what it is that we are going to get involved in, so there was a healthy debate—as there always should be—before you think about going to war."

— **General Colin Powell,** *Chairman of the U.S. Joint Chiefs of Staff*

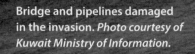
Bridge and pipelines damaged in the invasion. *Photo courtesy of Kuwait Ministry of Information.*

Palm trees and buildings destroyed by fire. *Photo courtesy of Kuwait Ministry of Information.*

Devastation at the Kuwaiti Airport. *Photo courtesy of Kuwait Ministry of Information.*

Every Glass Pane Broken

"We went into Kuwait City about three days after the Iraqi forces had been pushed out. It was still quite evident that there was mass destruction that took place. I don't think I saw a window that was intact in that entire city.

"Every glass pane was broken, cars and buildings were destroyed, and everything was in complete destruction. It was amazing. The oil wells were on fire, so there's this thick, black smoke everywhere, and you could hardly see a hundred feet in front of you with all the black smoke.

"That was a sad thing to witness, to see the destruction that took place in such a beautiful city."

— **Colonel Tyler Smith,** *Specialist, 22nd Support Command, Desert Storm*

mechanized brigades—rolling into Kuwait from multiple directions.

The lopsided math of the confrontation is staggering. At the time of the invasion, Kuwait had 16,000 troops in uniform. Iraq, on the other hand, fielded 955,000 troops in uniform, including many hardened veterans of the Iran/Iraq War, and 650,000 paramilitary troopers in the Iraqi Popular Army. In effect, Kuwait was outnumbered more than 60 to 1.

On paper, Iraq had one of the largest militaries in the world at the time:

- 5,500 tanks
- 3,000 artillery pieces
- 700 combat aircraft and helicopters
- 20 brigades of special forces
- 53 divisions

And the list went on.

And yet, in the initial clash with Kuwaiti forces, it was not the rout Saddam anticipated. In fact, had the Kuwaitis not run out of ammunition during the initial battle west of Al-Jahra, known as The Battle of the Bridges, it may well have been a Kuwait victory—at least temporarily. The Iraqis took losses and were forced to retreat for a time. At a minimum, brave Kuwaiti tank drivers slowed down the Iraqi advance, despite Iraq's superior numbers and superior firepower from multiple fronts. That temporary Iraqi retreat may have saved the Kuwaiti leaders from capture.

KUWAIT AIR FORCE: OUTNUMBERED BUT NOT OUT-FLOWN

At the time of the Iraqi invasion, Kuwait had 120 aircraft, including helicopters.

Iraq had 700.

In the first few hours of engagement—and despite a courageous and valiant response by available Kuwaiti Air Force officers—more than 20 percent of the Kuwait Air Force was lost or captured. While Kuwaiti pilots fought a brave and robust battle in the air, Iraqi commandos seized the major airports and the two military airbases. And though the Kuwait Air Force was prepared to attack and presented itself with honor, it no longer controlled its vital airbases. Kuwait's tiny Air Force was soon forced to retreat to Saudi Arabia. And within 12 hours of the first Iraqi units crossing the border, the invasion and occupation of Kuwait had begun. ◼

Life in the Embassy

"Marge Howell, the wife of Nat Howell, our ambassador in Kuwait at the time, organized family members in the Washington area. She had a network of everyone who had a relative caught in the American Embassy in Kuwait.

"They were able to send messages; we were able to get them in to talk on the phone. You can't imagine what it was like, if your husband or your wife is sitting there with 50 countrymen and hundreds of Iraqi soldiers outside the gate.

"Communications were critical not just for operational purposes but also for families. They would keep their morale up at the embassy, which was under siege. The embassy people got in contact with a number of their Kuwaiti friends who had stayed in Kuwait to smuggle supplies into the embassy: food, water, diesel, and gasoline. Ambassador Howell saw from the beginning that one of the possibilities could be a prolonged siege of the compound, so he stocked up.

"This included being sure the swimming pool in the compound was full of fresh water. We helped them perpetuate the myth that they were staying alive by drinking the pool water. Of course they weren't, because they had the foresight to bring in lots of bottled water, but that helped get their story out. 'Our intrepid garrison living on swimming pool water!' Their morale, their good humor, their resilience was just extraordinary. They were never grumpy, they were never whiny, they never complained. It was America at its best."

— **Ambassador Ryan Crocker,** *U.S. Ambassador to Kuwait (1994-97)*

Kuwaiti Air Force jet prepares for takeoff. *Photo courtesy of Kuwait Ministry of Information.*

Kuwaiti jet taxis on runway preparing for takeoff. *Photo courtesy of Kuwait Ministry of Information.*

Fighting that Mattered

"A Kuwaiti armored unit was able to deploy. If you look at a map of Kuwait, there's a town called Jahra and a road junction there—that was the critical link into Kuwait City. The Kuwaitis positioned themselves at that junction and held up the Iraqis until the Kuwaitis ran out of ammunition, out of tank rounds. That bought time for Kuwaitis who would have been killed, like the Amir, and the Crown Prince, and senior Al-Sabah family members—it bought them time to get out of Kuwait and into Saudi Arabia.

"It was just one of those little episodes—small in scale, not captured by the media—but it may have made the difference between the ability of the ruling family to get out, or to have been killed or captured. Had the latter happened, there might not have been any legitimate authority around which to build the later liberation of Kuwait. These small things matter in history."

— **Ambassador Ryan Crocker,** *U.S. Ambassador to Kuwait (1994-97)*

Overturned tank abandoned by
Saddam's forces on the battlefield
in Kuwait. *Photo courtesy of Kuwait
Ministry of Information.*

"We succeeded in the struggle for freedom in Europe because we and our allies remained stalwart. Keeping the peace in the Middle East will require no less. We're beginning a new era. This era can be full of promise, an age of freedom, a time of peace for all peoples. But if history teaches us anything, it is that we must resist aggression or it will destroy our freedoms."

— U.S. President George H. W. Bush

Oil fields set ablaze when Saddam's troops retreated from battle. *Photo courtesy of Kuwait Ministry of Information.*

Chapter 2

KUWAIT'S RESPONSE AND AMERICA'S COMMITMENT

"We choose our joys and sorrows long before we experience them."
— Khalil Gibran, Arab philosopher and writer

Human history is rarely made by the random acts of nature and geographic upheaval. In reality, such things are a mere backdrop to the true catalyst of history: human choice. These are the acts, courageous and cowardly, generous and brutal, which men and women make at key turning points in history.

On August 2, 1990, wise decisions of the brave and noble, as well as cruel deeds of the self-serving and brutal, would change the course of history. Quick thinking by key members of the Kuwait Amiri Guard, including young, respected officer Sheikh Fahad Al-Sabah, ensured that key members of Kuwait's leadership escaped to the safety of Saudi Arabia, as Saddam's designing web encircled, then smothered, the country.

Had Saddam captured Kuwait's Amir, Crown Prince, Prime Minister, and key Cabinet members, the Iraqi despot could have eliminated the legitimate leadership of Kuwait from the start, making it impossible for the nation to find an approved ruler around which to rally. These acts of human bravery and selfless sacrifice at great personal risk were what saved Kuwait as a sovereign nation.

In Washington, D.C., President Bush watched as Kuwait was overrun, then pillaged and plundered. The world turned its eyes to him for leadership. President Bush was determined from first learning of Iraq's invasion to get Iraq to withdraw from Kuwait—

peacefully through diplomacy and economic sanctions, or forcibly, as a last resort.

In effect, the course of history was determined by one man's hard choice to liberate Kuwait. In January 1991, after all other means had been exhausted, President Bush signed the National Security Presidential Directive authorizing the use of force with the United Nations approval.

THE CHALLENGE: HOW TO MOVE A MASSIVE ARMY A CONTINENT AWAY

Under siege, Kuwait had two major advantages often overlooked: determined and skilled leadership, and influential friends and allies. Also, Saddam had made the mistake (again, a pivotal choice) of invading a peaceful neighbor just as the Cold War was winding down. American forces in Europe were at peak combat readiness, but preparing to downsize and return home.

In such a changing geopolitical environment, the United States had the finest military in the world suddenly freed from European commitments. A logistical challenge remained, however: how to move a massive military machine from the forests of Central Europe to the sands of the Middle East—and do it yesterday. Land, sea, and air forces had to be deployed from the United States beginning that first week of August, as well as Coalition forces from member states who would contribute military forces. Coordinating and executing such a massive deployment was a major challenge.

Again, the solution was leadership—along with the vision and will to choose to right a cruel wrong and ensure that justice was done, even at a potentially high price. At the time, experts considered Iraq a formidable foe, on paper the fourth-largest military on earth, with recent combat experience in their long war with Iran. Whether the United States would lead a coalition of nations willing to fight for Kuwait was anything but certain.

GOVERNMENT IN EXILE

With the assistance and protection of Saudi Arabia, Kuwait set up a government in exile in Ta'if. There the Amir of Kuwait and his advisors began a global diplomatic campaign to counter the many lies issuing from the Saddam regime. In addition, the citizens of Kuwait were now scattered and confused. Some were living outside Kuwait, while others had stayed behind to challenge, or at least survive, Iraqi occupation.

Kuwait's exiled government officials had a daunting task—to take care of their people, both inside and outside Kuwait, and to rally the world in their defense. Such a task would take one of the most incredible diplomatic efforts in history, one that would eventually include a powerful 35-nation coalition led by the United States. Even the Soviet Union and China were persuaded to not block the United States and Kuwait's actions against Iraq in the U.N. Security Council. More incredible, perhaps, was President Bush's success in persuading Israel to stand down from fighting, even though Iraqi scud missiles would consistently attack the Israeli people.

THE ARAB SOLUTION

Not wanting this "squabble" to go beyond the Arab family, Arab leaders kept searching for *al-hal al-Arabi*— an Arab solution. Arab nations never appreciate outside interference. Arabs by nature are private, preferring to keep intertribal conflicts within the family. In the days following his invasion, Saddam was skilled in using that characteristic as a weapon to forestall any organized opposition to his occupation. This gave him more time to entrench in Kuwait, solidify his military and political control, and begin the elimination of the Kuwaiti people.

It soon became clear that Saddam had no intention of withdrawing from Kuwait. Still, as long as he appeared willing to accept some type of Arab solution, Saddam knew that Arab nations would be reluctant to accept any kind of international intervention. The Arab League, particularly, was stymied. While successfully rallying to produce several resolutions condemning Iraq and supporting Kuwait's claims, the Arab League was unsuccessful in mobilizing any kind of military response under its mutual defense pact.

League members needed a leader, one they could trust.

SADDAM'S IGNORANCE OF GLOBAL CHANGES

Perhaps the greatest failure on the part of Saddam was his inability to understand the monumental shift in the existing world order. The Soviet Union, Iraq's longtime ally and weapons supplier, was collapsing. Saddam had assumed that the USSR would continue to back him within the U.N. Security Council and stifle any efforts to condemn his actions. Saddam was blind to the revolutionary changes taking place: the significantly improving relations between Washington and Moscow, and the emerging Russian Republic with new political goals and objectives in the world. Saddam was so hopelessly cocooned behind his advisors, the very worst kind of "yes men," that he was never aware of the key geopolitical changes taking place in the world.

BREAKING WITH THE VIETNAM SYNDROME

When the Soviets did not oppose Coalition military intervention against Iraq, Saddam was distraught. He believed once more that he had been betrayed, that conspiracy was the only possible explanation. Additionally, Saddam did not understand what had happened within the United States. He believed the Americans still suffered from what was known as "The Vietnam Syndrome"—the inability to act militarily in far-off lands because Americans were still so traumatized by the Vietnam War.

To make matters worse, Saddam was convinced that the United States was involved in a nefarious plot to get rid of him. Consequently, Saddam viewed any attempt

Sheikh Saad Al-Abdullah Al-Sabah, Crown Prince of Kuwait, was forced into exile during the Iraqi invasion.
Photo courtesy of Kuwait Ministry of Information.

by the West to bring him to the negotiation table as suspicious at best.

THE ARAB STREET

Beyond that, Saddam also failed miserably in his estimation of just how much support for his invasion he could generate on the "Arab street." He looked to countries with a high concentration of ethnic Palestinian refugees, like Jordan, expecting that if America attacked Iraq, the Arab world would explode and fight off the "Crusader invaders." Saddam was banking on his popular support, which all his advisors continually assured him he had—a gambit that turned out to be hopelessly naive.

THIS WILL NOT STAND

When Saddam invaded Kuwait, President Bush and British Prime Minister Margaret Thatcher both happened to be in Colorado. They arranged a meeting and quickly determined that only a coalition of nations could remove Saddam's military from Kuwait.

The United States and the exiled Kuwaiti government launched a worldwide diplomatic effort to bring together a coalition to ensure that international law was enforced

LEFT & ABOVE: Devastation in and around Kuwait City from the invasion of Saddam's troops. *Photo courtesy of Kuwait Ministry of Information.*

His Highness the Amir of Kuwait Provides a Quiet Yet Powerful Example to the World

At the time of the Gulf War, Kuwait's present Amir, H. H. Sheikh Sabah Al-Ahmad Al-Jaber Al-Sabah, had been Kuwait's top diplomat, the Foreign Minister, since the 1960s. His skill at maneuvering sometimes unruly, even hostile, nations became legendary.

Over such a long and effective career, Sheikh Sabah became the icon of a skilled Kuwaiti cadre of diplomats. Sheikh Sabah knew instinctively where a tiny nation like Kuwait needed to place its diplomatic efforts that would pay the greatest dividends. He was particularly effective in working with the Permanent Members of the United Nations' Security Council. Speaking before the U.N., Sheikh Sabah said: "Kuwait's participation in international activities clearly indicates that our independence and our membership in the U.N. are not ends in themselves, but are rather a means by which Kuwait can share responsibility in improving the lives of the people in our country and in other countries." Through his long career, the Amir taught and supported peaceful coexistence and a solid diplomatic, cultural, and commercial cooperation.

Perhaps the greatest challenge in the realm of diplomacy comes with conflict resolution and in pushing diplomacy to the forefront of public policy. This takes a deft skill in balancing domestic, as well as foreign, interests. Sheikh Sabah took a lead role in founding and shaping the Common Ministerial Council for the G.C.C. and the European Union. This was essential to build the critical ties which make peace and prosperity such a great blessing to the people.

Sheikh Sabah is well known as a champion for freedom and self-determination and as a warrior against terrorism. He has stood time and again to demonstrate that Islam is not a religion of terrorism, but an organization that provides hundreds of millions hope in their lives and peace in their hearts. But when threatened, as Kuwait was on August 2, 1990, he became a lion in defense of his people and their rights. His efforts led to the Security Council's many resolutions against Iraq for its invasion and helped bring Kuwait to the forefront of world attention, leading to the passage of several key U.N. Security Council resolutions.

Later, the effects of the war, sometimes emotional and subtle, helped free and re-orient the Kuwaiti people and their government, once more shaped by the gentle, yet capable, hand of Sheikh Sabah.

Bombed signal towers show part of the damage done to Kuwait's communication infrastructure. *Photo courtesy of Kuwait Ministry of Information.*

Kuwaiti citizens struggle for food, water, and other supplies during the occupation. *Photo courtesy of Kuwait Ministry of Information.*

The President and the Prime Minister

President Bush went to Aspen after setting in motion the basis for U.S. and international strategy to liberate Kuwait. He held a National Security Council meeting, had discussions with regional leaders and Soviet leader Gorbachev, and gained a unanimous U.N. Resolution condemning the invasion. Then he and Prime Minister Thatcher held a joint news conference at Aspen.

"At about two o'clock, Margaret and I stepped out to a patio for a press conference. We condemned Iraq's aggression and called for a peaceful solution, with the withdrawal of Iraqi forces and the restoration of the Kuwaiti leadership. She put her finger on the most important point—whether the nations of the world had the collective and effective will to implement the resolutions of the Security Council and compel withdrawal and restoration. It would be up to American leadership to make that happen."

Bush, George H. W. and Brent Scowcroft. *A World Transformed.* New York: Knopf, 1998.

This Will Not Stand

On August 5, 1990, while meeting with the press on the south lawn of the White House in Washington, D.C., President Bush stated, "I'm not going to discuss what we're doing in terms of moving of forces, anything of that nature. But I view very seriously our determination to reverse out this aggression. And please believe me, there are an awful lot of countries that are in total accord with what I've just said, and I salute them. They are staunch friends and allies, and we will be working with them all for collective action. This will not stand. This will not stand, this aggression against Kuwait."

and justice served. In the fall of 1990, the U.N. Security Council passed multiple resolutions—first to enforce economic sanctions, then to authorize "all available means" unless Iraq withdrew from Kuwait by 15 January 1991—demanding the immediate and unconditional withdrawal of Iraq from sovereign Kuwait.

While Saddam had been a longtime ally of the Soviet Union, even that relationship was not enough to secure the USSR's support. Iraq found itself effectively alone and isolated in the world. Once again Saddam's paranoia grew as he watched the nations of the world side with Kuwait and the United States. He even resorted to offering payments to potential allies and backing a variety of regional political causes—anything it took to secure, somewhere, somehow, support for his annexation of Kuwait. In the end, he failed at every turn.

THE MILITARY OPTION—CHALLENGING THE OLD WAYS OF BUYING OFF THE ENEMY

There's an old Arab proverb of a shepherd who was losing one sheep each week to wolves. In desperation, he hired two big dogs to keep the wolves at bay. After some time, though the dogs kept the wolves back, the shepherd found that he was forced to slaughter two sheep each week just to feed the dogs. So he dispensed with the dogs and decided to "put up" with the wolves.

This proverb illustrates what took place in the lead-up to the Gulf War. For millennia, the Arab tribes and nations of the Middle East believed that the best way to control a dangerous enemy was to buy him off with "only one sheep" rather than engage in a fight that would cost two. Perhaps the greatest challenge, then, for both the government of Kuwait and President Bush, was how to convince the world that the only way to free Kuwait and bring peace and security to all nations was to prepare for war—a potentially costly war.

With such a mindset as a backdrop, the United States and Kuwait had a monumental task before them: trying to rally the Arab nations against a fellow Arab, one they believed should be bought off rather than confronted in war.

His Highness the Crown Prince Sheikh Nawaf Al-Ahmad Al-Sabah. *Photo courtesy of Kuwait Ministry of Information.*

Sheikh Nawaf, the current Crown Prince, helping in regional diplomacy with the former Amir Sheikh Jaber Al-Ahmad Al-Jaber Al-Sabah *Photo courtesy of Kuwait Ministry of Information.*

Shaping Kuwait Through Leadership

H.H. Sheikh Nawaf Al-Ahmad Al-Sabah is the Crown Prince of the State of Kuwait. The Crown Prince is nominated by the Amir, and then must be approved by the National Assembly in a majority vote of its members.

From Kuwait's independence in 1961, Sheikh Nawaf has served the Kuwaiti Nation in a variety of capacities. He was appointed Governor of the Hawalli District in 1962. Later he became Minister of Interior, Minister of Defense, and Minister for Social Affairs and Labor. In 1994, he was appointed Deputy Chief of the National Guard. In 2003, he was appointed Deputy Prime Minister, as well as Minister of Interior once again. He was the Minister of Defense during the invasion.

Sheikh Nawaf was skilled at implementing policies of teamwork in public and private ventures and initiatives and firmly believed that good teamwork was essential to the unity of Kuwait. He established the Private Contracts Department and created and refined the Legal Department in the Interior Ministry.

Sheikh Nawaf's ministry roles modernized and upgraded Kuwait's technology, helping to streamline government operations. He always stressed the importance of an open-door policy in government and management, he encouraged higher education for all ministry employees and provided them scholarships to local universities and colleges. Crown Prince Nawaf has been a strong advocate for coordinating security policy with other Gulf Cooperation Council member states.

Considered a steady and effective leader, Crown Prince Nawaf has worked behind the scenes for decades to help shape Kuwait into the economic, diplomatic, and cultural success it is today.

His Highness the Crown Prince Sheikh Nawaf working with the Kuwaiti military. *Photo courtesy of Kuwait Ministry of Information.*

H.H. Crown Prince Sheikh Nawaf as a diplomat for Kuwait. *Photo courtesy of Kuwait Ministry of Information.*

H.H. Crown Prince Sheikh Nawaf. *Photo courtesy of Kuwait Ministry of Information.*

WINNING SAUDI SUPPORT: LAUNCHING DESERT SHIELD

The greatest immediate challenge to the military option against Saddam lay with Saudi Arabia. Without gaining access to Saudi lands as a base of operations, Coalition forces could not mount a campaign against Saddam in Kuwait. On August 6, 1990, President Bush received a call from Secretary of Defense Dick Cheney, stating that Saudi King Fahd bin Abdul Aziz had agreed to a large contingent of U.S. and Coalition forces on Saudi soil. Now the military option was possible, and even more so, it had teeth. President Bush launched Desert Shield.

Once more the skill of those working diplomatically behind the scenes won the day. Immediately, the U.S. 82nd Airborne, select U.S. Air Force units, and U.S. Navy forces were on their way to the Gulf. This was perhaps the most decisive moment in the history of the war. And again a relatively small handful of people would either make or break the potential for victory over Iraq and the liberation of Kuwait.

Still, Desert Shield was purely defensive in nature. For now, the goal was to strengthen Coalition forces sufficiently to discourage Saddam's invasion of Saudi Arabia. Besides, the diplomatic mandate from the United Nations at that point was only to defend Saudi soil, while at the same time tightening up diplomatic pressure to convince Saddam to leave Kuwait. That was it. This was clearly an

President Bush meets with the late Amir of Kuwait, His Highness Sheikh Jaber Al-Ahmad Al-Jaber Al Sabah in the Oval Office of the White House to discuss the situation in the Arabian Gulf. *Photo courtesy of the George Bush Presidential Library and Museum.*

insufficient response, though many thought that was all that should be done. Neither Kuwait nor the Bush Administration, however, was satisfied.

THE POWER OF DIPLOMACY

On September 27, 1990, His Highness Sheikh Jaber Al-Ahmad Al-Jaber Al-Sabah, Amir of Kuwait, stood before the U.N. General Assembly in New York City and addressed the members:

> "I come here to tell you of the horrors and suffering we are enduring both inside and outside our occupied homeland, and to place before you our just cause," he said. "The fate of a people and of a nation are in your hands. Expecting you to act in good conscience . . . to win your endorsement . . . for our legitimate right to liberate our land. Furthermore, we trust that you will not waver in deciding on the measures needed to compel the invading aggressors to restore the legitimate authority and to put an end to their barbaric acts.
>
> "Iraq was bent on sweeping through the entire territory of Kuwait, violating its sovereignty and violating the sanctity of Kuwaiti citizens' lives and property. As a consequence, rape, destruction, terror and torture are now the rule of the day in the once peaceful and tranquil land of Kuwait. Hundreds of thousands of Kuwait citizens along with nationals of various other countries who were our guests have been made homeless and many of them have had their life savings robbed."

The Amir's speech completed, members of the U.N. General Assembly rose to their feet, offering enthusiastic applause that went on for some time. It was described by observers as "stunning." The assembly, by its response as a body and later individually, offered the Amir its support for the liberation of his country and the restoration of the legitimate state of Kuwait. Though it was apparent that prior to his speech the Amir had been discouraged, the U.N. response raised his spirits, as well as the outlook of the entire Kuwaiti delegation.

It was reported that, following his speech, the Amir was on the elevator with U.N. Secretary-General Javier Perez de Cuellar. "Your Highness," the Secretary General said, "I have been working at the U.N. for 12 years, and as an ambassador to my country just as long and I have seen nothing as strong as I witnessed today."

The Amir next traveled to Washington, D.C., to meet with President Bush at the White House. The Amir planned to relate to the president his personal knowledge of the crimes of pillage, rape, and plunder that Saddam was systematically carrying out in Kuwait. Prior to the meeting, the Amir had asked the Kuwaiti ambassador in Washington to send a suitable gift to President Bush. The ambassador chose a large, bronze map of Kuwait. When the Amir arrived at the White House, he could see that President Bush had the gift already mounted on the wall. The president thanked His Highness the Amir for the beautiful gift and asked what he could give him in return. The Amir paused, then said that any gift from the president should be for the Kuwaiti people. He pointed at the bronze map of Kuwait on the wall. The president understood. "Iraq will fail. Kuwait, free Kuwait, will endure," President Bush told him.

From the start, President Bush wanted to avoid committing ground troops because of the potential human cost. In his book *A World Transformed*, President Bush observed:

> "I think Cheney recognized early that sooner or later it would come to force. Dick was probably ahead of his military on this. No good soldier wants to go to war and would prefer instead to see all other options exhausted. Dick led the

Trust in President Bush

After meeting with President Bush, the Amir recalled, "When I spoke to President Bush, he looked at me and said, 'I will visit you in Kuwait.'" From that point on, the Amir felt a great relief. He trusted President Bush, perhaps more than any other world leader he knew.

Weapons used by Saddam's army.
Photo courtesy of Kuwait Ministry of
Information.

Hidden Diplomat

"The Kuwaiti Ambassador in Washington, D.C., Sheikh Saud Nasser Al-Sabah, was a very able diplomat and was incredibly active during this time with the Bush Administration, with Congress and with the American people, building support for what became the liberation of Kuwait. The Kuwait embassy stayed in touch with Kuwaitis as best they could through phone calls. The last thing we wanted to do was reach out from Washington to anyone in Kuwait, because if that call was monitored that would probably lead to a pretty severe Iraqi reaction. We left it to the Kuwait Embassy and to our diplomatic teams in Saudi Arabia, where the Kuwaiti government established itself in exile in the city of Ta'if, and in Washington with Ambassador Al-Sabah and his staff."

— **Ambassador Ryan Crocker**
   U.S. Ambassador to Kuwait (1994-97)

U.S. Soldier keeping watch from the open door of a Black Hawk helicopter. *Photo courtesy of NARA.*

way for the military, which I think is the model our Constitution envisioned: armed forces headed by civilians who were leading, not pushing, the military to understanding and fulfilling the missions set for them by the President.

"At the same time, our military never tried to avoid using force either, nor did they speak out against it. Colin Powell, ever the professional, wisely wanted to be sure that if we had to fight, we would do it right and not take half measures. He sought to ensure that there were sufficient troops for whatever option I wanted, and then the freedom of action to do the job once the political decision had been made. I was determined that our military would have both. I did not want to repeat the problems of the Vietnam War (or numerous wars throughout history), where the political leadership meddled with military operations. I would avoid micromanaging the military."

Excerpt from: Bush, George H. W. and Brent Scowcroft. *A World Transformed*. New York: Knopf, 1998.

On November 29, 1990, the U.N. Security Council presented and passed Resolution 678, calling for and authorizing the removal of Saddam's forces from Kuwait "by all means necessary." The resolution set the date of January 15, 1991, as the deadline for Saddam's withdrawal. ■

Nations Come Together

"This was a horrendous crime that was committed, and it was a crime that I think shook the countries of the world so that countries stood up and said, 'No, this is not going to stand. We are not going to allow this to move forward,' and they didn't. Countries came together and said, 'We are going to do something about it. We are going to reverse that.'"

— **Sheikh Salem Al-Sabah,** *Kuwaiti Ambassador to the United States*

Soviet Cooperation

"U.S. Secretary of State James Baker was on a trip—he had been in Moscow, and was in Mongolia when the invasion occurred. He got on a plane to Moscow the next day, asked for a meeting with Edward Shevardnadze, then the Soviet foreign minister, and said, 'Edward, we need to go out and make a joint statement condemning the Iraqi action.' Iraq was a Soviet ally, but the enormity of what Saddam had done and the strength of Baker's relationship with Shevardnadze got the Soviet foreign minister to do just that.

"The day after the invasion, there's the Soviet foreign minister and the U.S. secretary of state side by side, condemning the Iraqi action. And they just built from there. Baker made dozens and dozens and dozens of trips. President Bush was on the phone constantly, building international consensus. As President Bush had said 'This will not stand' four days after the invasion, he needed to get the necessary muscle behind his words.

"It wasn't just the Europeans, our traditional allies. The president worked with the Middle Eastern countries so that the coalition, the military coalition, eventually came to include not just Western troops but Arab troops. The Egyptians sent a division to Saudi Arabia, an entire division. The Syrians—and this is Hafez Al-Assad in Syria, no friend of ours—sent an entire armored division to join this coalition.

"This had never happened before, and the Bush Administration's ability to make it happen then is what spelled success for the entire endeavor. It was a success in the region because they went on to use that momentum to convene the Madrid Peace Conference late in 1991 where, for the first time, Syrians, Lebanese, Palestinians, and Jordanians sat down with Israelis in one room.

"That all grew out of that international coalition they were able to put together. As a career diplomat, that was the most stunning diplomatic achievement I have witnessed in my career."

— **Ambassador Ryan Crocker,** *U.S. Ambassador to Kuwait (1994-97)*

Kuwaiti women mourning the loss of
a loved one. *Photo courtesy of Kuwait
Ministry of Information.*

Chapter 3

THE HUMAN COST OF HONOR

One of the untold stories of the Iraqi occupation was Saddam's desire to annihilate an entire nation. He believed that for his plan to work, he had to erase the identities of the Kuwaiti people and replace them with Iraqis. To do this, he called upon his most trusted officers and confidants.

His strategy developed early on, prior to the invasion. He expelled Kuwaiti citizens and confiscated their documents—passports, identity cards, papers, and anything else a Kuwaiti citizen could use to prove his or her Kuwaiti ethnicity and nationality. Saddam's secret police developed a twofold approach: they gathered and eliminated all such documentation, both inside Kuwait and at the borders when any Kuwaiti attempted to leave the country.

In addition, Saddam's Mukhabarat, or secret police and intelligence officers, raided the Kuwait Ministry of Interior as well as the National Data Center, both located in Kuwait City, and collected all the records of Kuwaiti citizens for destruction. At the time, computer storage was mostly on site—transferring copies of data via the Internet wasn't yet done. The attempted destruction was a systematic effort that, if successful, would have made it almost impossible for the Kuwaiti government to prove who was in fact a Kuwaiti and who was not.

THE MIND OF THE TYRANT

Saddam understood that he couldn't just steal a whole country, especially not one as well-endowed as Kuwait. The country has the fifth- or sixth-largest proven reserves of oil in the world, generally cheap to lift and accessible. Kuwait is also located right on the sea, with excellent ports and easy access to tanker facilities where crude oil can be loaded by pipeline and shipped worldwide cheaply and efficiently. In essence, Kuwait was an organized and prosperous capital-generating machine, one that Saddam had lusted after for some time.

HONOR VS. SHAME

Another often-overlooked element influencing Saddam's invasion: the Middle Eastern desert tradition of enhancing one's honor among men while carefully limiting one's shame. For millennia, tribal leaders maintained their positions of power by building and protecting their individual and tribal honor. This was often accomplished when the men of one tribe raided another (usually weaker) tribe, plundering the vanquished to prove the true "man among men."

THE TRADITION OF THE RAID

In fact, when Saddam attacked Kuwait, many Arab leaders viewed the Iraqi invasion as Saddam's way of showing Kuwait's leadership—and the greater Middle East—that he was a powerful, virile man of honor, one not to be trifled with.

Most Arab leaders thought Saddam would make his point and then withdraw, taking what he wanted in plunder in true tribal fashion and thereby enhancing his nobility through the tried and true tradition of "the Raid." This was why most Arab leaders initially cautioned against militarily confronting Saddam over Kuwait. "He's just making his point," said both President Hosni Mubarak of Egypt and King Hussein of Jordan in so many words. "He'll go home."

Such an observation was, in fact, a valid one, especially considering the thuggish nature of a "Maximum Leader." The tradition of the raid goes back thousands of years, particularly in Arabia and surrounding regions. The prime objects of plunder were always, first, the women of the enemy tribe, then the livestock and other wealth and weapons, and finally anything else that was valuable.

Successful warriors would enhance their standing in the tribe. Why? Because raiding was a risky business. Sometimes you didn't come home. Enemies fought hard to protect their valuables, especially their women and children. A successful raider thus enhanced his honor not only within his own tribe but also with his enemies and rival tribes. What's more, tribes defeated in the raid were "shamed before God and men." While the tradition of the raid is an ancient one, the basic concept remains alive and well today in many parts of the world.

Saddam had squandered his nation's wealth on a horrendous eight-year war with Iran and was effectively broke; he also faced numerous challenges to his leadership and instabilities within his own country. Certainly Saddam saw Kuwait—the wealthy neighboring tribe—as a possible route to successfully enhancing his honor, filling his empty pockets, and feeding his starving people—especially his massive army.

THE SYSTEMATIC LOOTING OF KUWAIT: THE LAMB AND THE WOLF

For some time, Saddam had sought an excuse to invade Kuwait. His disjointed list of "complaints" against Kuwait included the alleged overproduction of oil, the fictitious stealing of Iraqi oil reserves, that both Kuwait and Saudi Arabia wanted Iraq to pay back its Iran-Iraq War debts, and Kuwait's supposed disrespect of Saddam himself. The list went on and on, often changing by the day, with his complaints coming fast and furious.

An old Arab fable illustrates Saddam's vindictive, irrational, even maniacal actions.

There was a lamb drinking by a stream. The wolf approached the lamb, stating, "You are polluting my stream, little lamb." The lamb pointed out that he was drinking downstream

from the wolf, so he was not fouling his water.

"Weren't you the one who threw dirt and sand in my eyes, disrespecting me last year?" the wolf said. The lamb calmly pointed out that he was not even born last year.

The wolf responded, "Well, the lamb that did it looked just like you, so it must have been your father or older brother who brought me shame." With that, the wolf pounced, devouring the lamb.

DOING WHAT THUGS DO BEST

Due to a history of endless war and government mismanagement, including allowing his family and his cronies to repeatedly plunder Iraq for years, and despite possessing some of the world's richest supplies of oil, Saddam Hussein had, in effect, purposely impoverished his own people.

The Iran-Iraq War ended within yards of where it started, and with up to a half-million Iraqis killed, the people of Iraq were spent. Their children were sick and dying, and most people—except for Saddam's family and tribe—lived hand-to-mouth, day after desperate day. Life in the streets of Baghdad was increasingly unbearable. Food shortages were endemic, medicines hard to come by. Saddam's insistence on maintaining the world's fourth-largest standing army was literally killing the nation of Iraq.

In a tyranny or dictatorship like Saddam's, all the major sources of income to the nation—such as oil, major businesses, weapons—are all controlled by the dictator and his cronies. Many tyrants such as Saddam converted those profits into cash, which was hoarded or shipped to foreign bank accounts, further sapping the nation's capital base. Money that should have been used for social programs and invested in companies that provide food, medicine, education, and jobs was being funneled instead into arming, equipping, housing, paying, and transporting the 1.5 million troops and a huge secret police apparatus. The greatest single cost of every dictatorship is always maintaining the army and secret police, whose first and foremost responsibility is to

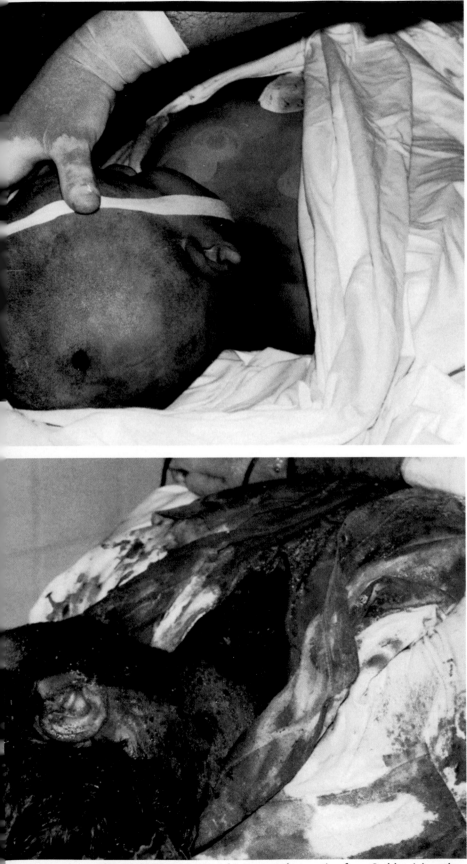

TOP & BOTTOM: Victims of torture and execution from Saddam's invasion.
Photo courtesy of Kuwait Ministry of Information.

Citizen Records

"The Kuwaitis put in a lot of effort to smuggle records—of who was a citizen and who was not—out of Kuwait to the government in exile. The fear was that Saddam would send people to populate Kuwait—people who would claim to be Kuwaitis but might not actually *be* Kuwaitis."

— **Ambassador Douglas Silliman**
U.S. Ambassador to Kuwait (2014 - Present)

keep the dictator in power.

Upon his invasion and occupation of Kuwait, Saddam systematically opened up Kuwait to pillage, rape, and plunder—in true tribal raid fashion. Foraging soldiers, many not fed or paid for months, were told, "Your pay is in Kuwait." Iraqi soldiers proceeded to empty Kuwaiti shops and stores, businesses and factories, schools and hospitals. Then they went after Kuwaiti homes. Finally, the soldiers stole garbage trucks and dump trucks, loaded them up, and shipped the plunder back to their families and friends in Iraq.

With no trucks or workers to remove garbage, refuse began piling up in the streets of Kuwait, which in the oppressive heat soon led to outbreaks of diseases that Kuwait had, prior to the invasion, effectively eradicated. In short order, the occupiers were turning a clean and orderly Kuwait City into a corrupt, mismanaged, dangerous, and filthy Iraqi city, complete with new diseases, failing businesses, nonexistent municipal services, unnecessary food and medicine shortages, and general chaos and collapse.

In essence, a society that had invested its oil wealth in smart, effective technologies, quality management, social programs, and a solid infrastructure found itself rapidly deteriorating into the identical creature that had infected it.

The invading Iraqis captured and killed

members of the Kuwaiti resistance, leaving their bodies in the streets and warning Kuwaitis to not provide burial services for their dead. Despite this danger, families would sneak out at night, breaking curfew to dig hasty graves and bury their honored loved ones.

THE KNOCK ON THE DOOR

Kuwait is a family-oriented society, where hospitality to honored guests is considered a moral and social obligation. But under Saddam's occupation, it became a huddled, suspicious, fearful society where all families lived with the terror of a knock at the door in the middle of the night, a knock that too often ended with Saddam's dreaded Mukhabarat taking away a beloved family member, who would never be heard from again.

THE TACTIC OF RAPE

But the knock on the door wasn't the Kuwaitis' only fear. Many times soldiers shot the people for their cars. Peaceful demonstrations and protests against the occupiers ended with the Iraqis opening fire on

Affecting World Economy

One little-recognized side effect of the Iraqi invasion was its impact on the poorer nations of Africa and Asia. Kuwait was financially supporting 70 underdeveloped countries, and the upheaval of the invasion shut down or delayed those assistance programs. Namibia even sent a representative to the United Nations to report the hardship that Saddam's occupation had caused for that country. In addition, the invasion raised the price of oil and generally caused instability in international markets, hurting poorer nations the most.

Saddam's Vengeance

"When I saw Saddam killing our people and torturing our girls and boys, I expected that Saddam would do anything to destroy Kuwait. So, surely, it was not a surprise for us to see, when Saddam was driven out of Kuwait, 730 Kuwaiti oil wells blown up and on fire. But, of course, that's Saddam's way of destroying Kuwait."

— **Saud Al-Nashmi,** *Drilling Operations Manager, Kuwait Oil Company*

Street market destroyed in the invasion. *Photo courtesy of Kuwait Ministry of Information.*

Parking garage destroyed
by bombing and fire.
*Photo courtesy of Kuwait
Ministry of Information.*

THIS PAGE & OPPOSITE: Images of destruction at the Kuwait International Airport. *Photo courtesy of Kuwait Ministry of Information.*

the demonstrators. Saddam's cronies often encouraged rape as a tactic of intimidation and an attempt to destroy the Kuwaiti family unit. A woman raped was humiliated before her family, but the woman wasn't the only one affected by the horrific act. The culture of honor and shame dictated that the men of that family were weak and shameful creatures because they were unable to protect that which was most precious to them.

Men, women, and children were often raped as part of Saddam's method of torture and interrogation in a horrible system of breaking down the emotional strength and will of individuals. The use of electrical shock and mutilations were also the interrogators' preferred methods of torture.

THE HORROR OF THE UNKNOWN

Although most Kuwaitis—as well as those from other nations caught in occupied Kuwait—were not subjected to such atrocities, life still became increasingly intolerable and uncertain. Everyone knew someone who had been arrested, interrogated, and tortured, or someone who had simply "disappeared." The continual, unrelenting stress of occupation took its toll as people began to realize that help was not on the way—at least not for a while.

As life deteriorated, the Kuwaiti people began to wonder not "what shall we eat" but "whether we will eat at all." Kuwait became a nation of prisoners who increasingly feared what lay before them—the horrible unknown.

Where once women were private, safe, and protected behind the *hijab* (the traditional veil or scarf head-covering), now women no longer felt safe, not even in their own homes. In short, the known fears of invasion and war were replaced by the even greater terror of the uncertainty of each new day and the increasing lack of value Saddam's occupiers placed upon human life. ■

Torture

A Kuwaiti tells of his arrest, torture, and interrogation:

"The day after very intense and heavy interrogation, where most of us were tortured, the Mukhabarat asked us to make a TV interview [for propaganda purposes].

"They were angry at the Kuwaitis. I was a Kuwaiti. When they changed us from one location to another they always said, 'Where is the Kuwaiti?' and they'd come and the guards would take turns beating me. Once you are blindfolded and handcuffed, they take the handcuffs and then put them behind you so your whole body is exposed and you are blindfolded. It's absolutely dark. You don't know, but you can imagine, how many people are asking different questions, and you don't know who is doing it to you and standing next to you to torture you. They have many different tools, and they are experts [at it].

"How do you survive the hunger, the torture, the inhumane way they treat you, not enough sleep, food? You have to keep strong and have faith in God. For me, I would not think about the negative things so I wouldn't be too low and sad. I would never think about my family, because I knew that would bring a lot of tears. So I would think about the positive things in life, though they took turns beating me with rifles and kicking me, especially when they got mad because their building was bombed."

The Knock at the Door

"The day Iraqi soldiers walked into Kuwait, on the afternoon of August 2, 1990, our guard informed us that soldiers were at the doorstep asking for Mr. Morad Yusuf Behbehani, my father.

"When we told them that Mr. Morad was away from Kuwait traveling, they asked for the next responsible person in the household. My uncle, Mr. Mohammed Saleh Behbehani, came forward and identified himself to the Iraqis.

"The soldiers told my uncle, Mohammad, that they needed to ask him a few questions and took him outside beyond the courtyard. We waited for a long time for Mohammad to return and then went out of the compound to look for him. When we could not find him anywhere nearby, the neighbors across from our house informed us that they had seen Mohammad being driven away by the soldiers in a vehicle.

"We began searching for our uncle all around the city but could not find him, nor did we receive any information for quite some time. It was much later when we learned that Mohammad was taken by the Iraqi Army to Baghdad. There he was held in prison until Kuwait was liberated by the U.S. military in February 1991. My uncle suffered in prison, doing whatever he could to survive the ordeal. It was only when the Iraqi forces left Kuwait and retreated north towards Baghdad that they released Mohammad Saleh Behbehani and let him return to his family in Kuwait City."

— **Ali Morad Behbehani**, *Kuwaiti citizen*

Street in Kuwait City destroyed. *Photo courtesy of Kuwait Ministry of Information.*

THIS IMAGE & RIGHT: Scenes of destruction at Kuwait Parliament building caused by the invading force. *Photo courtesy of Kuwait Ministry of Information.*

A fire set by Iraqi forces during the invasion.
Photo courtesy of NARA.

Fire damage to the Kuwait Airways headquarters building in Kuwait City. *Photo courtesy of Kuwait Ministry of Information.*

Damaged business in Kuwait City. *Photo courtesy of Kuwait Ministry of Information.*

The Martyrs Monument in Kuwait City. *Photo courtesy of Brandon Young, RMS.*

Chapter 4
THE KUWAITI RESISTANCE

The 20th century produced the most significant accomplishments of mankind—human flight, medical discoveries, the rise of living standards, space travel and exploration, and countless others.

Unfortunately, the last century also saw the worst wars in human history—with their accompanying genocide, destruction, disease, and human tribulation on an unprecedented scale. Perhaps worst of all, the century saw the creation of horrible weapons of mass destruction that are now proliferating throughout the world. Humankind now faces the real possibility of global annihilation.

One 20th-century event, however, stands as a shining example of worldwide cooperation and brotherhood in the face of brutal tyranny: the liberation of Kuwait. United as one in a noble cause, the world of nations, even longtime enemies, came together to accomplish something that had never been done on such a scale.

And on the individual level, the liberation of Kuwait provided the perfect example of what a few determined patriots can do to right one of the great wrongs of history. Labeled "the Kuwait resistance," these patriots all lived for one objective: to free Kuwait.

THE THREE OBJECTIVES OF THE RESISTANCE
Hastily formed in occupied Kuwait, the leadership of the Kuwaiti resistance soon identified three primary objectives:

1) Secure and preserve Kuwait's national citizenship records and archives to ensure that Saddam did not achieve his nefarious goal to erase the identities of Kuwaitis.

2) Encourage as many Kuwaitis as possible to remain in the country until Kuwait could be liberated. To do this, the resistance had to be capable of protecting and helping both Kuwaiti citizens and foreign national guests who remained in occupied Kuwait.

3) Demonstrate to the world that Kuwaitis were not just passive observers but actively engaged, where possible, in frustrating the occupiers' objectives, making it difficult for them to gain control of the country.

In accomplishing these objectives, the resistance would also raise the morale of the Kuwaiti people and give them hope.

It's important to remember that Kuwait is a flat, open desert with no caves, forests, or mountains where Kuwaiti resistance could hide. The only cover available was the city: inside homes, shops, and other places where civilians lived. Resistance leaders knew that any attacks on the Iraqi occupiers would result in the possible execution of innocent people, along with the destruction of Kuwaiti homes, businesses, and any property that could be tied to resistance acts of assassination or sabotage.

All over Kuwait, men and women came together in groups or cells committed to a single overarching goal: resistance. Occasionally, individual cells organized around a well-known individual, a leader such as Sheikh Ali Al-Sabah, a member of the royal family, who then established an operational command structure to better target the enemy and protect civilians.

FREE KUWAIT!
For obvious reasons, the resistance operated independently with little communication between—or even knowledge of—other Kuwaiti groups or cells. Although separated by circumstance and levels of skill and experience, and always vastly outnumbered and

Meeting Schwarzkopf

"After the war, I had the honor of meeting with General Norman Schwarzkopf when he visited Kuwait with his family. General Schwarzkopf told me that the information the Coalition received from the Kuwaiti resistance was priceless, accurate, and highly useful."

— **Mahmoud Hamad Al-Dosari,** *Kuwaiti resistance fighter*

Letter from General Horner to Kuwaiti Resistance Leader

Letter from General Charles "Chuck" A. Horner, U.S. Air Force, Commander of U.S. and allied air operations during the Gulf War, to Mohammad Al-Faresi, Kuwaiti resistance leader, after the liberation:

Dear Mohammad,

I cannot thank you enough for the leadership you provided during the war to liberate Kuwait. As an airman, you flew your share of combat missions against the invaders, but also as the vital link with the brave men of the Kuwaiti resistance, you made it possible for our air power to be targeted against the evil people in occupied Kuwait City. You inspired all of us in the air operation center, and we shared your grief for your nation and your enjoyment during our victory. The night the Iraqis left Kuwait was the finest moment in my life, and I was so proud to serve with you in making that happen.

Sincerely,

General Chuck Horner

Asrar Al-Qabandi

One of the bravest yet unsung heroes of the war was a young woman—Asrar Al-Qabandi.

Though she had many opportunities to flee Kuwait, Asrar refused and instead joined the resistance, helping trapped foreigners and Kuwaitis escape; smuggling weapons, medicine, and food to the elderly and disabled; stealing and hiding Iraqi weapons; and planning attacks against the occupiers.

Prior to the Iraqi invasion, Asrar was a schoolteacher, working with the disabled and autistic. All who knew her were impressed by her quiet courage and kind, serving heart. She was caught by the Iraqi Mukhabarat and taken to a torture center. For more than a month, she was abused and brutalized as the enemy tried to get her to reveal others in the resistance.

Asrar's body, stuffed into a plastic bag in typical Mukhabarat style, was dropped on the front doorstep of her father's home, an ax blade imbedded in her head.

To many Kuwaitis, the story of Asrar Al-Qabandi has become a legend, though she paid the ultimate price for the honors and accolades she received posthumously. More importantly, she's become a symbol of the power of one woman to make a difference in what many thought was a hopeless situation. She showed great courage, inspiring many to rise up and follow her to victory. And perhaps the most important lesson she ever taught was the power each individual has to make a difference.

Armed Kuwaitis provided resistance to Saddam's forces during the occupation. *Photo courtesy of Kuwait Ministry of Information.*

inadequately equipped, each cell's mission was the same: free Kuwait.

These courageous individuals sniped enemy combatants, especially officers; laid explosives to destroy, disrupt, or capture convoys of Iraqi ammunition and weaponry; and bought and stole weapons from the Iraqi military. They smuggled to safety the national citizenship records of the Kuwaiti people, ensuring that Kuwaitis would be able to counter Saddam's lies about the citizenship of Kuwaiti residents.

A HIGH PRICE TO PAY

On the morning of February 24, 1991, the Al-Messilah resistance cell had planned an attack on a group of Iraqi forces south of Kuwait City. Tragically, they were surprised by an Iraqi patrol. The ensuing clash became known as one of the Gulf War's most heroic engagements in which the resistance fought to the death.

What began as bad luck—the unexpected arrival of a group of Iraqi soldiers passing by on routine patrol of the Al-Qurain neighborhood—resulted in an unwinnable situation where the Kuwaitis knew they had to make a hard choice.

At that time, Saddam had directed his soldiers in Kuwait to:

1) Burn and blow up all homes which displayed resistance slogans, the Kuwaiti flag, or pictures of Kuwait's leadership,

2) Burn and demolish every neighborhood in which any Iraqi military, security, or Iraqi Popular Army soldiers were ambushed and killed,

3) Arrest any person who owned or was found possessing a firearm, and

4) Break up and destroy any anti-Iraqi demonstrations by force.

The Iraqi patrol moved closer and closer to the safe house of Al-Qurain armed resistance and its large weapons cache. The Messilah fighters had to decide whether to surrender or fight. They

Bombed location of battle between invading forces and Kuwait resistance called the Al-Massilah group. Location is now home to the Al-Qurain Martyrs Museum, a memorial for those killed during the Iraq occupation. *Photo courtesy of Kuwait Ministry of Information.*

Brave Youth

"The resistance was Kuwaiti people from all creeds and all families. It was across the board. It was a lot of young guys and young girls that were very, very brave and did a lot of brave things, and a lot of them lost their lives. A lot of them were captured and killed. They suffered and sacrificed greatly. They are our heroes."

Sayed Hadi Mohammed Alawy was the leader of the Al-Messilah Kuwait Force, a resistance group whose 31 young members had moved its weapons to Al-Qurain, where the risk of detection was thought to be less. They even wore a uniform of sorts, designed by Sayed—a T-shirt with the name and motto of the group. Were the circumstances and events not so lethal, one might mistake them for a college fraternity, rather than a serious group of underground fighters."

— **Sheikh Salem Al-Sabah**, *Kuwaiti Ambassador to the United States*

chose to fight, though they knew this was not a battle they could win.

Only 19 members of the Messilah group were present at the safe house in Al-Qurain when the firefight broke out, and they were armed with only small-caliber weapons. During the 10-hour battle, the Iraqis brought in reinforcements and heavy weaponry, including tanks. A coordinated Iraqi attack with tank fire blew out the windows of the safe house, destroying the staircases and crumbling the building's foundation. Of the 19 resistance fighters, 12 were killed in the battle and 7 captured, most of them badly injured.

THE Al-QURAIN MARTYRS MUSEUM

The Al-Qurain safe house stands today as a memorial to the slain. It is preserved as a museum and monument to the resistance fighters, to their honor and sacrifice, and to record for future generations how bravery is sometimes overwhelmed by brutality.

What was once a place of defiant rejection of the unjust attack on Kuwait has become a quiet gathering place, a pilgrimage site for those who desire to honor the men and women who made the ultimate sacrifice. The Kuwaiti resistance is generally an unheralded movement. Practically no one outside of Kuwait even knows these cells existed during those dark days in 1990

and 1991. Time, apathy, and new generations have a way of erasing important pieces of history.

Still, the message these dedicated few sent to the occupiers will remain forever etched into the hearts of every Kuwaiti, and in the hearts of those in the Coalition who fought with them. They were in touch with the exiled government in Ta'if, continually coordinating their activities.

After the liberation, General Norman Schwarzkopf visited the Qurain Martyrs Museum. "When I am in this house," he said, "it makes me wish that we had come four days earlier. Then, perhaps, this tragedy would not have happened."

WAS THE RESISTANCE NECESSARY?

Was the resistance necessary? Were the sacrifices worth it in the end? Such questions are hard to answer when looked at purely from a tactical standpoint. But in the hearts and minds of the Kuwaiti people who suffered the brutalities and hopelessness of the occupation, such heroes made a tremendous difference. In the end, to a nation unjustly brutalized, these resistance fighters brought a quiet but lasting pride and inspired a burning gratitude. Such are the quiet, often forgotten things that make a land a home—and a piece of desert ground a nation. ■

Widespread looting by Saddam's soldiers occurred during and after the invasion and occupation of Saddam's military force.
Photo courtesy of Kuwait Ministry of Information.

Citizens collect water during the occupation.
Photo courtesy of Kuwait Ministry of Information.

Kuwaiti resistance helped drive Saddam's forces out of Kuwait. *Photo courtesy of Kuwait Ministry of Information.*

The late Crown Prince Sheikh Saad Al-Abdullah Al-Sabah. *Photo courtesy of Kuwait Ministry of Information.*

Heroic Resistance

"The Kuwaiti resistance fighters were heroic against an unimaginably brutal enemy who would kill them in a way you wouldn't want to even contemplate.

"They gathered intelligence, they communicated intelligence, they carried out operations against the Iraqis throughout the entire occupation. The U.S. Embassy was very careful in reporting these things, saying things like, 'There was an incident last night in which an Iraqi army vehicle was ambushed, and everyone in it was killed.' And we would officially comment, 'Oh, that's interesting.' But clearly what they were telling us was that the resistance had made a successful hit."

— **Ambassador Ryan Crocker**
   U.S. Ambassador to Kuwait (1994-97)

Mission Strategy

"Our cell wasn't just focusing on the military side of it. We were focusing on what we call passive resistance, including how to help the Kuwaiti people hold their ground and how to keep the chain of supply flowing with food, electricity, water, and medical supplies. Our leader assigned one guy who was responsible for providing support for civilians.

"It was a real challenge when you are fighting among civilians. You need to protect the civilians, you need to protect their kids, you need to protect their elderly. You have hospitals full of injured, and you need to protect them also. We focused on not only the fighting side—we also focused on the humanitarian side, which was our mission too.

"Our intent was not to target the Iraqi civilians who had come to support their army. Our mission was clear. We targeted critical command and control, critical military forces, what we thought to be military targets. We never harmed civilians. Our mission was mixed between military and humanitarian support.

"Our aim was also to provide intelligence and exact information. They sent dozens of telecommunication devices for us, operated through a satellite system. Our strategy was to provide information on every single enemy position in Kuwait. When the Coalition was going to target the enemy, they needed precise locations; they didn't want to harm civilians. Knowing the precise locations, the coordinates, was very important to them."

— **Mohammad Al-Faresi,** *Kuwaiti resistance*

Embassy Protection

"The people in Kuwait City were amazing. In the chaos of the invasion, they got what word they could out to the American community, a number of whom had come to the embassy to take refuge. You had a handful of diplomats, but dozens and dozens of private American citizens who were sheltering in the embassy. The embassy was besieged. For a while there, we didn't know if the Iraqis would come in or not.

"You had a handful of U.S. Marine guards with light weapons. If they had to, they would have used those weapons to defend the compound as best they could. Fortunately it didn't come to that, but day to day they didn't know, and we didn't know, if the Iraqis would change their minds and just put a tank through the main gate.

"It was a tense situation, but that American flag stayed up during the entire occupation and became a true symbol to the Kuwaitis who were still in the country that the United States was with them."

— **Ambassador Ryan Crocker**
U.S. Ambassador to Kuwait (1994-97)

Protecting Prisoners

"Our aim was to protect even the Iraqi soldiers who surrendered to our resistance, because you must protect them when they are prisoners of war. If anyone surrendered, we protected him and put him in a safe house until he was handed over to Coalition forces. This was our aim. We are proud, really, as one of the many major resistance groups, that we saved thousands of Iraqis. We protected them; we gave them food, supplies, and medical treatment. Then we personally handed them over to Coalition forces as prisoners of war."

— **Mohammad Al-Faresi**
Kuwaiti resistance

Kuwaiti citizens show resourcefulness in acquiring water during the occupation.
Photo courtesy of Kuwait Ministry of Information.

Young Kuwaiti boy transfers a large tub of water back to his family during the occupation. *Photo courtesy of Kuwait Ministry of Information.*

A BGM-109 Tomahawk land-attack missile rises into the air after being launched from the aft vertical launch system aboard guided missile cruiser USS *Bunker Hill* (CG 52) during Operation Desert Storm. *Photo courtesy of NARA.*

Chapter 5

FORGED IN THE CAULDRON OF WAR

Led by the United States, an international coalition gathered to oppose Iraq—first in principle, then ultimately by force of arms. In November 1990, when diplomatic efforts had failed to resolve the dispute and convince Iraq to depart from Kuwait, the United Nations set a deadline for Saddam to withdraw, authorizing the use of "all necessary means" to confront Iraq in the event Saddam failed to comply.

WAR BEGINS

Saddam Hussein did not comply with U.N. Security Council sanctions, and on January 17, 1991, American, British, and allied air power from the international coalition launched a massive campaign of missile strikes, bombing, and shelling from offshore ships. Everything available from air and sea was thrown at Saddam's forces. Later, this would become known as the famous "Shock and Awe" campaign.

Lighting the night sky over Baghdad and Kuwait, Coalition air power pounded the Iraqi positions in an unprecedented display of aerial bombardment. This was also the first war in which ship-launched cruise missiles were deployed and smart bombs guided to their targets from high above. Pinpoint, precision weapons the world had not seen before were all in action over the skies of Kuwait and Iraq.

STORMIN' NORMAN, LEADING THE COALITION

President Bush chose a bear of a man to lead Coalition forces. General "Stormin'" Norman Schwarzkopf had commanded CENTCOM (U.S. Central Command)

since November 1988. General Schwarzkopf had lived in the Middle East as a youth while his father was stationed in Iran for the U.S. military, so he understood the necessity of dealing effectively with different cultures and peoples. He was a skilled and effective general who was devoted to his troops, and a solid choice to lead soldiers into battle.

"THE MOTHER OF ALL BATTLES"

Saddam Hussein, always one for hyperbole, liked to tell the world that the war with the American and Coalition forces would be "the mother of all battles" if President Bush was "foolish enough" to try to kick him out of Iraq's 19th province—which is what he called Kuwait. Of course, once the Iraqis went head-to-head with the Americans and her allies, the "Maximum Leader's" finest divisions lasted only a few days. The mother of all battles it was not.

Indeed, it was one of history's most lopsided defeats. Before the ground offensive even began, air power alone caused thousands of Iraqi soldiers to desert and destroyed more than 1,000 artillery guns, 1,300 Iraqi tanks, and 900 other armored vehicles. The air campaign was so effective that Iraqi forces in Kuwait were starved for supplies from Iraq—Coalition aircraft had decimated Iraqi command and communication centers, destroyed ammunition storage facilities, almost entirely eliminated Iraqi navy vessels and air force aircraft, and attacked and destroyed three-quarters of Iraq's electrical power-generating capacity.

THE AIR WAR: JANUARY 17

This highly coordinated, massive U.S.-led air attack

Fear of a Partial Withdrawal

"Our greatest fear going into the fall [1990] was that Saddam would withdraw from Kuwait City. There's a terrain feature north of the city called the Mutla Ridge, and we feared he would withdraw to that ridge, keeping control of the northern Kuwaiti oil fields. And if he did that, the effort to assemble an international coalition to expel him from Kuwait would have gone from very difficult to pretty much impossible.

"If the Kuwaitis got their capital city back, we feared that the international community would say, 'That's good enough.' That was my biggest nightmare going through October and into November: a partial Iraqi withdrawal. That would have probably been good enough to stop Coalition military action against him in the fall. But by January, it would not have been good enough."

— **Ambassador Ryan Crocker**, *U.S. Ambassador to Kuwait (1994-97)*

Black smoke pours from burning oil at an offshore oil terminal near Kuwait City. *Photo courtesy of NARA.*

Expectations

"Iraq had a very large army at over a million strong, which they could field at some level. I think they had a paramilitary force of another 500,000 or so. It was a mammoth army. We understood that the Republican Guard Divisions—at least five, I believe—were the absolute cream of the Iraqi Army. In the deployment, Saddam kept them back, in what we would call an operational strategic reserve. His front lines were made up of his other units, and they were not well-equipped.

"That was what we really knew. In our war games, which we ran based upon computer models, some of the answers we got on that were pretty scary. We could expect a long fight, and we could expect a high number of American casualties, in the 10,000 to 20,000 range."

— **General (ret) Dennis Reimer**
U.S. Army Deputy Chief of Staff, Operations and Plans, Desert Storm

Patriots vs. Scuds

"The other unsung system was the Patriot, an air defense system [anti-ballistic missile system]. Saddam Hussein had Scuds [missiles]. They weren't that accurate—they terrorized more than they killed. Still, people were fearful of the Scud attacks. We had just developed the Patriot, but we had not yet used it operationally in warfare."

— **General (ret) Dennis Reimer**
U.S. Army Deputy Chief of Staff, Operations and Plans, Desert Storm

Patriot Missile System.
Photo courtesy of Raytheon.

commenced on January 17 at 2:38 a.m. (Kuwait time), first targeting Iraq's air defense systems. With those neutralized, the Coalition shifted to targeting communications networks and facilities, then weapons plants and oil refineries that produced military fuel.

And it did not end there. The Coalition attack, known operationally as Desert Storm, would be fought in the air for more than a month, destroying thousands of Iraqi targets with the latest cruise missiles, laser-guided bombs, stealth bombers, and cutting-edge night-vision capability.

The Iraqi Air Force quickly got the message that going head-to-head in the air against the Americans was suicide. Iraqi pilots turned their planes around, many seeking safety by flying into Iran, or they kept their aircraft grounded throughout the war.

U.S. strategic planners understood that the kind of war Saddam wanted to fight was in the open desert, head-to-head with armor and artillery. Saddam envisioned commanding one mighty, final, decisive battle where his thousands of Russian-made tanks and artillery pieces and hundreds of thousands of men would swarm and overwhelm the Americans and British, awarding him the grand, honored victory of which he had always dreamed.

The Americans, of course, had no intention of fighting Saddam's army on his terms. The air war was designed to degrade Saddam's massive military, destroying its morale and limiting its capacity to fight long before the coalition ground war even began. Air power did just that.

THE BATTLE OF KHAFJI, A POLITICAL TURNING POINT: FEBRUARY 1

In all great conflicts of history, there are key turning points. The Battle of Khafji was such an engagement. From the beginning of the Coalition air campaign, Saddam believed that air power alone could never decide this war—so he determined to goad the Coalition into a decisive land battle.

Trying to force the Americans to engage, Saddam first shelled Saudi port facilities, launching Scud ground-to-ground missiles into Saudi Arabia and even into Israel, hoping to draw the Coalition and Israel into a massive land war. He believed that once Muslims and Arabs everywhere could see his troops fighting and dying on TV at the hands of the Americans, the Muslim world would rise in anger and rush to his defense.

This tactic, of course, was delusional. The Coalition had suffered minimal losses and held back patiently, refusing to engage on the ground—even after Iraqi troops opened Kuwait's oil storage facilities and dumped 200,000 barrels per day of crude oil into the Arabian Gulf.

Finally, after being assaulted by 2,000 sorties every day, and desperate to confront the Coalition on his terms, Saddam ordered his forces to invade Saudi Arabia on January 29. Attempting to attack the border town of Khafji, Iraqi troops bulldozed their way in with the 1st and 5th Mechanized Divisions and the 3rd Armored Division—and ran up against U.S., Saudi, and Qatari forces. The U.S. Marines and U.S. Army Rangers, backed up by Coalition air sorties, repulsed the attack.

By February 1, 1991, after American artillery and Coalition air power pounded the Iraqi troops, two Saudi National Guard battalions and two Qatari tank companies retook Khafji. The battle was an excellent example of the joint use of modern ground multi-national forces combined with U.S. air power. The city of Khafji was liberated at a cost of about 40 Coalition dead and 50 wounded. The Iraqis lost between 75 and 300, with an estimated 400 Iraqis taken prisoner.

The Iraqi troops' incursion into Khafji became a strategic rallying point and one of the most important battles of the war. Saddam's single penetration into Saudi territory was the proverbial last straw. Any reluctance that the Saudis might have had to use military force to drive Saddam from Kuwait was now gone.

"FIRSTS" OF MODERN WARFARE

President Bush determined to commit the full might and weight of a well-established, superior American military. For the first time in the history of warfare, cruise missiles would be launched from U.S. warships at sea.

Another "first" of the campaign would be the successful shooting down of a number of Iraqi Scud missiles using the Patriot Missile System. The effectiveness of this guided, anti-ballistic missile system was seen around the globe as cameras embedded in the missiles broadcast images to American and international television audiences. This was also a first.

President Bush provided yet another first on November 8, 1990, when he announced the "no-notice deployment"

of U.S. VII Corps. Already forward-deployed in southern Germany, the VII Corps would now be focused on a new enemy, in a distant location, in entirely different terrain conditions. Deploying "already deployed" units with all their equipment and ammunition to another theater of operations had not been done since WWII. Although it's routinely done today, this was new in 1990. The VII Corps initiative also involved leaving family members in Germany as the military personnel deployed to the Middle East. The VII Corps was transitioned from essentially a defensive European Cold War mission to a potentially offensive mission in the Arabian Desert. This was also a first in U.S. Army military annals.

New technologies were fielded as well, such as Global Positioning System (GPS) devices—mostly handheld then, but a forerunner of the current mounted position-locators.

Global Positioning System (GPS)

"Army Space Command called one time and said, 'We got these little handheld global positioning systems (GPS) that are lightweight.' They were called SLGRs [Small Lightweight GPS Receiver]. I said, 'Send all your SLGRs over to Schwarzkopf.' At the end of the war, some Iraqi prisoners asked, 'How did you find your way around in this desert? This is our backyard and we're always lost.' The SLGR was a technology champion in that particular war. It was what made a difference—the people knew where they were. That allows you to get accurate fire, it allows you to get air support. It allows you to do a passage of lines in the middle of the night like they did. Those are tricky maneuvers. If you don't know where you are, then you're not able to do that."

— **General (ret) Dennis Reimer,** *U.S. Army Deputy Chief of Staff, Operations and Plans, Desert Storm*

The Patriot Missile System provided a dome of protection against Saddam's Scud missiles. The Patriot, designed by Raytheon, intercepted Scuds in the sky before targets reached the ground. *Photo courtesy of Raytheon.*

General Norman Schwarzkopf, Commander, U.S. Central Command, waits to welcome prisoners of war released by the Iraqi government upon their arrival at the Riyadh Air Base during Operation Desert Storm. *Photo courtesy of NARA.*

Cousins Don't Attack Cousins

"We obviously understood that the Kuwaitis were all in favor of what we were doing. It was obvious at the beginning to most—and this goes back to the politics and the complexities of the life and the culture of Saudi Arabia and the Arabian Peninsula—but there was still some reluctance on the part of the Saudis to believe this could really be happening. 'Cousins don't attack cousins! We don't attack our fellow Arabs!' But I think by the time we came up to, and particularly after, the Battle of Khafji, they were then convinced this had to be done, and that this was the right thing to do."

— **Lieutenant Colonel (ret) Jim Janda**
   U.S. Senior Operations and Intelligence Advisor to Saudi Arabia National Guard, Desert Storm

The General

"Norman Schwarzkopf was a brilliant general, but he was no diplomat. His temper was legendary, and that was probably a very good thing. Leaving the diplomacy to President Bush and Secretary of State Baker had successfully built the Coalition. Now it had to function as a fighting machine, and that required a certain Schwarzkopf 'firmness.'"

— **Ambassador Ryan Crocker,** *U.S. Ambassador to Kuwait (1994-97)*

Chemical Weapons

"Our number-one concern was the Iraqi use of chemical weapons. Were they going to use chem, and, if so, against whom and what type of agent? We were scared to death of that. Anybody in their right mind would be. That was our greatest focus.

"We'd interrogated some artillery battery commanders. We knew there were chemical munitions on their site and they had permission to fire chemicals on us, but they had just not done it. The nearest we could tell from talking to them is they figured we were pissed off enough already. They didn't want to make us anymore angry than we already were.

"Still, we had 10,000 body bags at Fort Bragg, North Carolina, shipped to the Gulf that we expected to use, mainly because of Iraqi chemical weapons."

— **Major (ret) Roger Perkins**
   Intelligence Officer, U.S. Army Special Forces Command, Desert Storm

Uncertainty

"We knew Saddam Hussein had chemical weapons. We knew he had used them on his own people and on Iran. There was so much uncertainty surrounding the whole conflict that we, as young soldiers, had no idea what to expect.

"Very different from what we have now going into Afghanistan or other theaters of operations. We've been there long enough that we know what to expect. This war was different. We were entering into an area of great uncertainty."

— **Colonel Tyler Smith,** *Specialist, 22nd Support Command, Desert Storm*

Members of Sea-Air-Land (SEAL) Team 8 and French commandos hang from a Special Patrol Insertion/Extraction (SPIE) rope secured to a helicopter during Operation Desert Storm. *Photo courtesy of NARA.*

Desert Storm also saw the first major combat use of the Abrams Tank and the Bradley Fighting Vehicle, both of which performed most effectively when placed in the hands of superbly trained soldiers.

SHAKING THE DESERT

While these firsts of modern warfare were being tested and successfully applied, a number of older—perhaps a bit haggard, but still proven—weapons systems were seeing what would be their last forays into battle.

Dean Stephens, a gunner's mate on USS *Missouri*, recalls that few in active service had experience targeting and firing the battleship's 16-inch guns, weapons so huge their blast would shake the desert and raise dust and flame hundreds of feet in the air.

"I don't suppose we'll see a battlefield exercise like that again," Stephens observes. "But a Marine unit was

Trust

"Right before we attacked, I was busy explaining our scheme of maneuver to a group of soldiers. One of the sergeants stopped me and said, 'Don't worry, General. We trust you.' My throat closed over. I could barely answer because in an instant that NCO captured essentially what we're trying to do as a leader: earn and sustain that trust in the way we go about leading those entrusted to our command. All the operation was about trust. In the end, after the liberation of Kuwait, it was trust in our Armed Forces and in America."

— **General (ret) Fred Franks**
Commander, VII Corps, Desert Storm

ABOVE: Aviation ordnanceman removes cover from the AIM-9 Sidewinder missile prior to loading on an A-7E Corsair II. *Photo courtesy of NARA.*

A U.S. Army M-1 Abrams tank during Operation Desert Storm. *Photo courtesy of NARA.*

Reconnaissance

"Our special operations forces were in there weeks before the invasion went off. We were already in, looking at what was going on. We also had contact with the Kuwaiti resistance inside Kuwait City and were working with them. We'd been preparing for this a long time. The ground forces going in really just brought the hammer to the nail.

"There were different agents who would go in and do dead-drops [clandestine operations] and retrieve information. We used whatever means were available to us. Some of it was just people coming across the border and telling us information. We had people on the ground with radios who were also talking back and forth."

— **Major (ret) Roger Perkins**
Intelligence Officer, U.S. Army Special Forces Command, Desert Storm

We Are All Army

When completely deployed, VII Corps had 21,000 U.S. Soldiers and 23,000 British Soldiers from U.S. Reserve Components, 19,000 in Army Reserve or National Guard, and 2,000 in individual ready reserve. These soldiers and leaders were essential to the success of Desert Storm.

"This was a total force. In other words, it involved all three components of the U.S. Army. We were eating dinner one night. There were probably 10 or 15 soldiers, and General Carl Vuono [U.S. Army Chief of Staff] had taken his staff over there to be with the soldiers. He asked the troops, 'Okay, how many of you are Army Guard? And how many of you are Army Reserve?' But before anybody could answer, he said, "It doesn't matter. We're all U.S. Army.'"

— **General (ret) Dennis Reimer**
U.S. Army Deputy Chief of Staff, Operations and Plans, Desert Storm

pinned down on a hillside, calling for targeting that was at our maximum range. We warned them there could be a short round or two . . . but nevertheless, we came in right on the mark."

Stephens shakes his head as he remembers what was called for—and delivered. "I don't think there are any of the old battlewagons left now, but we did a job in Kuwait."

The job that certainly got done resulted in the destruction of hundreds of targets in a matter of hours. This included ship bombardment, ship-fired cruise missiles, and fighter planes and bombers from the United States, Great Britain, Kuwait, and Saudi Arabia flying more than 116,000 sorties during the first six weeks of the war, dropping more than 85,000 tons of bombs.

THE RUSE

As the air war was winding down, Coalition forces shifted tactics, focusing their air attacks primarily on Iraqi forces occupying Kuwait and southern Iraq. Operation Desert Saber—a multi-front ground campaign headed by the Americans and the British—punched into Kuwait from the south.

Meanwhile, the U.S. Marines appeared to be launching a huge amphibious attack from

the Arabian Gulf. Of course, this was a ruse. Schwarzkopf stationed U.S. Marines offshore with landing craft and naval forces, their eyes on the Kuwaiti beaches. This led Saddam to think that the Americans would charge ashore from the east with landing craft and naval bombardment—as U.S. forces did on Iwo Jima, and as Marines are trained to do.

In reality, the main Coalition attack would sweep around from the northwest, engaging the elite Iraqi Republican Guard divisions from their flank in a massive surprise attack.

THE GROUND WAR: FEBRUARY 24

The initial attack from the south was pure diversion, designed to take Iraqi attentions off the main thrust, which swung around through the desert from the west out of Saudi territory, penetrating western and southern Iraq.

U.S. VII Corps commander Lieutenant General Fred Franks ordered the 1st Cavalry Division to conduct feints and demonstrations in the Wadi Al-Batin area, in what was termed the Ruqi Pocket. They accomplished this mission superbly. Along with the 11th Aviation Brigade, the 1st Cavalry Division launched deep Apache AH-64 attacks and continuous VII Corps artillery raids against Iraqi positions. This deceived the defending Iraqis from detecting the main Coalition attack launched almost 100 kilometers west.

Because of the early success of U.S. Marine Corps units, General Schwarzkopf directed LTG Yeosock to determine if the Third Army (comprised of VII Corps and XVIII Corps) could attack early. LTG Fred Franks of VII Corps and LTG Gary Luck of XVIII Corps agreed and quickly adapted earlier plans.

For the VII Corps, coming from the green fields and pleasant forests of Europe, the desert took some adjustment. That morning, a massive *shamal* sand storm had blown in from the northwest. High winds pelted troops and equipment with blinding sandstorms, limiting visibility.

Shamal winds can lift many tons of desert dust to a lofty height, obscuring the sun and sandblasting man and machine. These fierce winds from the northwest can easily blind someone, and anything mechanical is often so badly fouled in the storm that it grinds to a halt.

Taking a knee from the desert heat. *Photo courtesy of NARA.*

Deceiving the Enemy

"Before we deployed to Saudi Arabia, we published a training plan for the coming quarter that would allow us to adapt our maneuver techniques to the desert and to the mission we expected to get. It took several weeks for us to arrive in the Northern Desert but once we had, we were ready to train.

"The 2nd Armored Cavalry Regiment arrived in Saudi Arabia early in December 1990 as the first VII Corps unit to deploy from Germany. Our first mission was to screen a sector 80 kilometers wide to the south of the Kuwaiti border and north of the only east-to-west road in the Northern Desert—the Trans-Arabian Pipeline Road, known as "Tapline Road." Part of the reason for being there was to deceive the Iraqis as to where VII Corps would be positioned. In fact, the attack would take place over 200 kilometers west of our first area of operations."

— **Lieutenant General (ret) Don Holder**
Commander, 2nd Armored Cavalry Regiment, Desert Storm

Marines of the 1st Marine Expeditionary Force (MEF) move across the desert in a training exercise. *Photo courtesy of DOD.*

Smoke and Sand

"The day of the main attack was the worst day of rain and blowing sand. We were moving through a tremendous *shamal*. If you can imagine on the side of a vehicle about an inch of sand being caked, blown like concrete against your vehicle—it really was the worst weather I've ever seen.

"At the same time, Saddam Hussein had set all Kuwaiti oil wells on fire. You could not see the sun in Kuwait—it was that bad. The smoke and over-hanging pollution, all that black smoke and dark, gloomy skies."

— **General (ret) John H. Tilelli**
Commander, 1st Cavalry Division
Desert Storm

Crossing the Berm

"At that time, we didn't know how long this was going to last. We had no idea. The estimates for casualties were 10,000 and above—the casualty count was huge, but we didn't know. We were using figures from World War II. We knew this was going to be a serious fight.

"It was night by the time we actually got ready to cross the berm. It was very dark, but there was enough light that you could see the two sand berms that had been constructed along the border—huge, very high. You could see light gleaming off them and I remember passing through with my eyes wide open. In the distance, I could see the missiles going off and I remember thinking 'rockets' red glare, bombs bursting in air.'"

— **Brigadier General (ret) Anne Macdonald**
Brigade Adjutant, Aviation Brigade,
1st Armored Division, Desert Storm

But the U.S. troops were prepared. Anticipating the storm, they had installed special improvised filters on tanks and other equipment, giving them a huge advantage over the enemy. After the battle, Iraqi defenders would express amazement that the VII Corps' thrust was so effective in such debilitating weather.

In the afternoon of February 24 at 1500, some 11 hours earlier than planned, the Third Army attacked.

The Iraqis had moved close to 30 divisions in and around Kuwait. They had hundreds of thousands of combat forces alone in Kuwait and southern Iraq. These were not Saddam's elite forces, however.

Once Kuwait had been occupied and pacified after the initial Iraqi invasion, Saddam had pulled back his elite Republican Guard divisions and replaced them with poorly trained and badly equipped regular Iraqi units. His elite units moved north across the Iraq-Kuwait border and dug in. Saddam placed his deadliest forces in an arch from the Gulf through southern Iraq, west to the Saudi border. There he waited, daring the Americans to take him on in the open desert.

SADDAM REMEMBERS AMERICA'S FAILURE IN VIETNAM

Saddam cared little for the common Iraqi soldier, believing that he could take many times the number of casualties the Americans could before they would give up and go home, he said, "as they did in Vietnam." He wanted a bloodfest in the desert, one that would bog down his enemy and hand him victory. He built countless bunkers and dug long trenches filled with oil and gas, and planned to flame them into an inferno to "welcome" the Coalition fighters, which he labeled crusaders.

So that is exactly what General Schwarzkopf let Saddam think: that Coalition forces would come straight at him through Kuwait, hit him in the desert with a frontal assault, and then run right into his trap—an Iraqi-armored gauntlet.

THE LEFT HOOK: FEBRUARY 25

On the afternoon of February 25, 1991, LTG Fred Franks, VII Corps Commander, had a quick orders group meeting at a forward desert location. There he made the decision to execute "Fragplan 7," one of seven contingency plans developed to adapt the VII Corps attack to the enemy and terrain after the attack began. That plan turned the VII Corps 90 degrees east and opened an attack lane to the north for LTG Gary Luck's XVIII Corps.

After the war, VII Corps named that maneuver "the Left Hook," and journalists picked up the term. Previously discussed and "war-gamed," the plan was quickly set in motion in a continuous three-division armored-fist rolling attack.

On February 26, just two days after the ground war began, VII Corps rapidly sliced through Saddam's finest armored and infantry divisions. Colonel Don Holder's 2nd Armored Cavalry Regiment (ACR) attacked to destroy the security zone of the Iraqi Republican Guard Forces Command (RGFC) Tawakalna Division in the Battle of 73 Easting. LTG Butch Funk's 3rd Armored Division rapidly turned east to complete the destruction of the Tawakalna Division on February 26-27, while MG Ron Griffith's 1st Armored Division turned 90 degrees east and destroyed the majority of the RGFC Medina Division. MG Tom Rhame's 1st Infantry Division made a night forward-passage of lines through the 2nd ACR to complete the destruction of the Tawakalna Division and major elements of the Iraqi Jihad Corps.

Meanwhile, Colonel Johnnie Hitt's 11th Aviation Brigade attacked deep beyond the 2nd ACR with AH-64 Apache helicopters, adding to the destruction of Iraqi Jihad Corps and Iraqi units attempting to flee the theater. At the same time, Major General Rupert Smith's 1st British Armored Division completed passage through the minefield breech cleared by the U.S. 1st Infantry Division. The 1st British destroyed the Iraqi 52nd Armored Division and other Iraqi units in their swift attack to the east to Highway 8, north of Kuwait City.

The strategy opened an attack lane east for LTG Gary Luck's XVIII Corps. COL Doug Starr's 3rd Armored Cavalry Regiment, MG Jim Johnson's 82nd Airborne Division, MG "Binnie" Peay's 101st Airborne (Air Assault) Division, Major General Michel Roquejeoffre's 6th French Light Armored Division, and MG Barry McCaffrey's 24th Division all simultaneously engaged Republican Guard units in their sector of the now "Third Army attack east."

Despite the Iraqis' familiarity with the land, they never saw the attack coming. Thousands were killed, and hundreds of armored vehicles destroyed. Apparently they never knew where the stealthy divisions of what became known as "the Left Hook" actually were.

In fact, captured Iraqis expressed amazement that the Americans were able to navigate through the desert so effectively, especially at night. Some admitted that while they had lived in the region all their lives, they couldn't match what the Americans had done in one of the worst deserts on earth. Of course, the United

Renewed Allied Cooperation

For the first time since WWII—when they fought together in the desert of North Africa—British, French, and American forces cooperated as allies in Desert Storm. The 1st British Armored Division was placed under tactical control of U.S. VII Corps, and the 6th French Light Division was placed under tactical control of VXIII Corps. The Brits named their participation Operation Granby, while the French called theirs Operation Daguet.

One Traffic Cop

"The operations would have been confusing except [General Charles "Chuck"] Horner was in charge. He was the traffic cop for the whole thing—he was able to integrate all of it. The Royal Saudi Air Force is pretty large. The Brits were there in large numbers. There were smaller but meaningful contributions by the French, the Australians, the New Zealanders. In all, about a dozen air forces were involved. There was not one instance of fratricide—nobody on our side ever got shot down by anybody else on our side. Very unusual and only possible if you have one guy leading the band."

— **General (ret) Merrill "Tony" McPeak**
Chief of Staff, U.S. Air Force (1990-94)

Explosive ordnance disposal in Kuwait. *Photo courtesy of DOD.*

A Marine armored vehicle crewman wears a nuclear-biological-chemical (NBC) protective mask. *Photo courtesy of NARA.*

Desert Smart and Desert Tough

"We got a briefing from General Schwarzkopf on our general plan of operations—we were going to be the main attack, so we had a lot of planning considerations. Focus our training. We wanted to get to what we called 'desert smart' and 'desert tough.'

"We had to learn how to live in a desert. We had to learn some long-range gunnery skills, and the maneuver of large-formation skills. We began to get that new global positioning system (GPS). We hadn't seen any of that before. The Army went out and procured a limited number of those, so most of our maneuver formations had the GPS system so we could navigate in the desert."

— **General (ret) Fred Franks**
Commander, VII Corps, Desert Storm

The Left Hook

"The strategic intent of the Left Hook was to minimize the devastation of Kuwait City. The intent was to hold the Iraqis' attention on the Marines and the Army coming up from the south. Once the Iraqis were surrounded, they'd realize they were trapped, and they would try to retreat very quickly. The plan worked pretty well. The devastation to Kuwait City from combat was minimal. No coalition rounds were fired into Kuwait to get the Iraqis to leave. They were already beginning to flee to the north, and so they ran right into us. We destroyed an awful lot— about three of the elite Republican Guard divisions were completely wiped out.

"There were more Republican Guard units in Baghdad, however, who stayed to protect Saddam. Our plan worked. We unhinged their defense, and with them rattled and surrounded, they left or tried to leave. Therefore, the devastation in Kuwait during combat, during the 100 hours, was minimized. There certainly was lots of devastation before that, however, from what the Iraqis had done as they invaded and looted and stole things away to Baghdad."

— **Major General (ret) John Macdonald**
Squadron Operations Officer,
2nd Armored Cavalry Regiment, Desert Storm

States had help—a newly invented technology known as GPS, or global positioning system.

The Left Hook engagement was the first time that U.S. ground forces had fought the infamous Republican Guard. Starting on February 26 and over the next two days, Coalition forces proceeded to systematically decimate parts of Saddam's finest divisions.

SCUD MISSILE ATTACK IN KHOBAR

But while their forces were being annihilated up north, the Iraqis launched a Scud missile on February 26 that landed in Al-Khobar, Saudi Arabia, near Dhahran. The missile struck a U.S. Army barracks, killing 28 and wounding 98. The barracks housed, among others, the 475th Quartermaster Group, an Army Reserve unit from Farrell, Pennsylvania.

That attack was the worst single loss of the war. News reports covering the destruction of the barracks also showed families gathering at the local VFW meeting hall in Pennsylvania, seeking more information about their soldiers, while neighbors and friends consoled those who had lost loved ones. It was a tragic day of the war, and it took a heavy toll.

Baghdad Radio called the American dead "cowardly traitors" who "mortgage the sacred places of the (Arab) nation," a reference to having American "infidel invaders" occupy sacred Islamic ground. Saddam made this declaration, hoping that the Muslim world would condemn the Saudis for inviting the Americans onto the holy lands of Islam, "occupying Islam's heartland with unbelievers."

Throughout the war, Saddam's propagandists used every possible angle to attempt to swing the Arab and Muslim worlds into the Iraqi camp, accusing the Americans and the Coalition of every horrible deed imaginable, including blasphemy against Islam. Saddam was never successful, however, primarily because most of the Muslim world knew who he really was.

LIBERATING KUWAIT

In the meantime, a U.S. Marine expeditionary force moved north out of Saudi Arabia, supported by an all-Arab corps of Saudis, Kuwaitis, and Egyptians. The force smashed Iraq's forward defenses, advancing so quickly that the Iraqis remaining in Kuwait could not muster an effective counterattack.

Coalition forces pressed into Wafrah, then Jahra, and finally into Kuwait City. While some Iraqi units caught in Kuwait

Scouting Basics

"I conducted 2ACR's covering force operation as a movement to contact. My tactical concept was to move as quickly as possible without over-extending the Regiment, to detect the enemy early with air scouts and other means, to hit him with long-range weapons first and then to close on important positions with tanks and Bradleys. That worked well in the fair weather we'd experienced in our training. When sandstorms blew in, grounding air scouts and blinding close air support, however, we reverted to cavalry basics of thorough ground scouting supported by prompt, heavy fires from tanks and artillery."

— **Lieutenant General (ret) Don Holder**
Commander, 2nd Armored Cavalry Regiment,
Desert Storm

A close-up view of an HH 46A Sea Knight from Helicopter Combat Support Squadron 5 (HC-5) as it hovers over a ship while conducting a vertical replenishment during Operation Desert Storm. *Photo courtesy of NARA.*

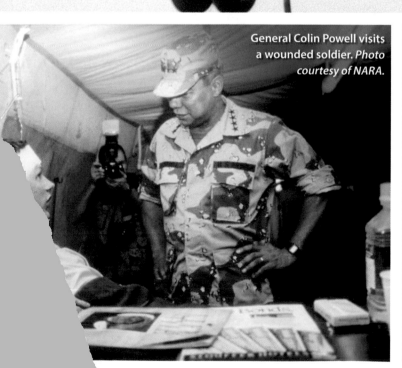

General Colin Powell visits a wounded soldier. *Photo courtesy of NARA.*

World-Class Army

"We attacked at the Wadi Al-Batin, which was to present a feint or decoy, making the Iraqis think that the main effort was going to go straight up to Kuwait. That's when we lost our first soldiers, the first day of the feint.

"Any credit on the success of this thing, Desert Shield and Desert Storm, has to go to a world-class army, an army that was well trained, an army of great men and women who served our country and died for this nation. And they went there with the express purpose to kick Saddam Hussein out of Kuwait. They knew that the way to get the mission done was to get that job done, and come home."

— **General (ret) John H. Tilelli**
Commander, 1st Cavalry Division, Desert Storm

cKenzie County
Public Library

A close-up view of the markings on the side of an A-7E Corsair aircraft from Attack Squadron 72 (VA-72). Each camel represents a combat mission flown by the pilot during Operation Desert Storm. *Photo courtesy of NARA.*

An AV-8 Harrier jet is launched from the flight deck of amphibious assault ship USS *Nassau* (LHA-4) in the Gulf of Oman. *Photo courtesy of NARA.*

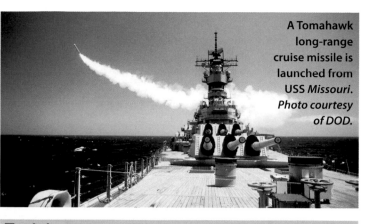

A Tomahawk long-range cruise missile is launched from USS *Missouri*. *Photo courtesy of DOD.*

U.S. troops wearing M-17A1 field protective masks on the perimeter of their camp. *Photo courtesy of NARA.*

Ready for Conflict

"The commanders and soldiers of the BRO [Big Red One, 1st Infantry Division] were fully trained and ready for this conflict. They could maneuver, they had precise gunnery skills, and they had the American will to win. These superb skills, combined with the modern technology of our equipment, produced a decisive victory. The Iraqi Army was clearly unprepared to do war with this group of BRO soldiers. They fulfilled our motto: No Mission too Difficult, No Sacrifice too Great, Duty First."

— **Lieutenant General (ret) Tom Rhame**
Commander, 1st Infantry Division, VII Corps, Desert Storm

Training and Teamwork

"I wanted to hit them with a closed fist, and rapidly attack through the Republican Guard, and also open a lane for the XVIII Corps north of us, and destroy the Iraqi Republican Guard Forces Command in our sector of attack, which our units were successfully doing. As one of the mothers of an attacking 2nd Cavalry trooper said, 'It was training and teamwork that kept my son alive.' It was that training, that 'toughness,' and that skill and courage of the soldiers. I was so very proud of them, and continue to be so today."

— **General (ret) Fred Franks**
Commander, VII Corps, Desert Storm

Training

"Before we deployed to Saudi Arabia, we published a training plan that would allow us to adapt our maneuver techniques to the desert and to the mission. It took several weeks for us to arrive in the Northern Desert, but once we had we were ready to train.

The Regiment arrived in Saudi Arabia early in December 1990 as the first VII Corps unit to deploy from Germany. Our first mission was to screen a sector 80 km wide to the south of the Kuwaiti border and north of the only east-to-west road in the Northern Desert—the Trans-Arabian Pipeline Road, known as "Tapline Road." Part of the reason for our being there was to deceive the Iraqis as to where VII Corps would be positioned. In fact, the attack would take place over 200 km west of our first area of operation.

We occupied that sector for over a month, screening a 100-kilometer front by air and ground patrols while we acclimated the soldiers to the desert and to train. Our training provided platoons, troops, companies, and squadrons with time, fuel, and ammunition. We rehearsed the mission at Regimental, squadron, and troop/company levels."

— **Lieutenant General (ret) Don Holder**
Commander, 2nd Armored Cavalry Regiment, Desert Storm

Weapons of Mass Destruction: The Game Changer

Weapons of mass destruction (biological agents, poison gas, and nuclear weapons) had spread into the Middle East during the 1980s. Saddam had bought, developed, and fielded them in his war against Iran. These horrible and unpredictable weapons had the power to dramatically change the face of battle, and the reality of these weapons forced Coalition leaders to change how the war would be planned and executed.

fought well, most of Saddam's forces were badly trained, poorly supplied conscripts who suffered from low morale and had no desire to die for Saddam Hussein. Many surrendered and were taken prisoner.

Despite horrible weather conditions—rain, wind, dust, and mud—the Coalition, led by Kuwaiti units, liberated Kuwait City on February 26. U.S. forces continued to sweep through major swaths of southern Iraq, clearing much of the desert to a point south of Nasiriya. The rapid advance of the Coalition ground forces quickly demoralized the enemy and mercifully ended the war in only 100 hours. Baghdad radio suddenly announced on February 26 that Iraq would honor the requirements of U.N. Resolution 660 and withdraw from Kuwait. Soon Iraq agreed to submit to all U.N. resolutions.

CONFRONTING THE ELITE REPUBLICAN GUARD: FEBRUARY 27

But while Kuwait City had been liberated, thousands of Iraqi troops were still on the offensive in the desert. On February 27, the U.S. VII Corps spotted Al-Medina, Saddam's most elite Republican Guard tank division, named after a sacred city in western Saudi Arabia where the Prophet Muhammad is buried. Iraqi tanks were spread out about 20 kilometers across the breadth of the front lines. Right away, U.S. tankers

Modern American Warfare

"Other battles would be more destructive than 73 Easting. Other units would fight with the same proficiency demonstrated by Holder's dragoons. Yet in this first major engagement against the Republican Guard, the U.S. Army demonstrated in a few hours the consequences of 20 years' toil since Vietnam. Here could be seen, with almost flawless precision, the lethality of modern American weapons; the hegemony offered by AirLand Battle doctrine, with its brutal ballet of armor, artillery, and air power; and, not least, the élan of the American soldier, who fought with a competence worthy of his forefathers on more celebrated battlefields in more celebrated wars."

Excerpt from: Atkinson, Rick.
Crusade: The Untold Story of the Persian Gulf War.
New York: Houghton Mifflin Harcourt, 1993.

Misdirection

"The plan was to make Saddam believe that we were going to come in from the sea with the Marines and from the south in Saudi Arabia, right straight up the highway into Kuwait, and we built an entire false information operations campaign. General Schwarzkopf did a great job doing that. We executed maneuvers from the sea, we practiced going ashore in front of TV cameras so that Saddam stayed with his guns pointing to the south and out onto the Arabian Gulf.

"Then, very quietly—I'm not sure how you do this quietly—we moved two corps (100,000 troops) out along Tapline Road, well to the west, so that we could be set up and maneuver all the way around the Republican Guard and slip in from the direction they were not expecting. We went north, well out into Hafar Al-Batin in Saudi Arabia, and then hooked around the enemy.

"Part of the force cut off any reinforcements coming down from Baghdad. With that maneuver, we crossed the berm and stopped, and then started again and stopped, and started again and then went around. The cavalry regiment's purpose was to knock out all the initial defenses and reconnaissance so that the main body, the 1st Armored Division and the 3rd Armored Division, could make the turn and then slam into the flank and destroy the Republican Guard. We did just that."

— **Major General (ret) John Macdonald**
*Squadron Operations Officer,
2nd Armored Cavalry Regiment, Desert Storm*

An airman helps to move ordnance containers during Operation Desert Storm. *Photo courtesy of NARA.*

Fighter jets fly over Kuwaiti oil fires.
Photo courtesy of DOD.

The Experience of Vietnam

"We had all been young leaders in Vietnam. If given the opportunity to make changes, we were not going to let a lot of the things that happened in Vietnam happen while we were in charge.

"During the 1980s, we rebuilt the discipline of the force, not only in integration by putting minorities into key positions, but building the proper culture and the vital trust and confidence in the overall force—all an outgrowth of the negatives of Vietnam. We had dealt with a lot of those frustrations, and my contemporaries were determined that we were going to put Vietnam in the rear-view mirror with Operation Desert Storm.

"I think that was a big part of the psyche during that period. The Vietnam experience molded all of us in one way or the other, and from my generation, those failures created a strong determination to change."

— **General (ret) Ronald Griffith**
Commander, 1st Armored Division, Desert Storm

began destroying Iraqi tanks, one after the other, without taking any U.S. casualties.

The 1st Armored Division fought methodically, destroying tanks from more than 3,000 meters out at Medina Ridge and elsewhere. To their south, the 3rd Armored Division and 1st Infantry Division were also engaging and destroying Iraqi RGFC and other units in a three-division fist. Though the Iraqis returned fire, they could not range the Americans. Within a relatively short time, it was obvious that this battle, and probably the war, wouldn't last long.

Starting on February 26, Coalition forces proceeded to systematically devastate parts of Saddam's finest divisions. Lightning speed, close and deep air attacks, massed armored combined-arms maneuvers, skilled and courageous soldiers, and the ability to engage the enemy from an unexpected direction all proved beyond the capabilities of Saddam's Republican Guard armored divisions to handle.

Within hours, many of the Iraqis found themselves overrun and cut off from the possibility of retreat or escape. Leaving the Iraqi desert, the Americans began to squeeze those Iraqi units caught in the middle in southern Iraq and Kuwait. The sweep was unprecedented. An almost impossible logistical and operational feat, the VII Corps moved through some of the most inhospitable land on earth with thousands of armored vehicles, helicopters, and support units, all rolling as one massive, coordinated juggernaut through a surprised and bewildered enemy. Although outnumbered, the Corps engaged and destroyed 11 Iraqi divisions, including several key Republican Guard divisions.

OUTGUNNING SADDAM'S BEST IN 100 HOURS

In the end, Saddam's armored units were completely surprised and quickly overwhelmed. Elite Iraqi Republican Guard divisions attempted to make a stand but were decimated by February 27. In all, an estimated 10,000-20,000 Iraqi soldiers,

An F-14A Tomcat from Fighter Squadron 114 (FF-114) flies over a battlefield in Operation Desert Storm. *Photo courtesy of NARA.*

Like Water Through a Screen Door

"Of course, being in the 11th Cavalry, you watch the 2nd Cavalry very closely. They were the eyes and ears of the VII Corps. Of course, we were the eyes and ears of V Corps, so you're watching this unfold and witnessing how good we were. I had tank platoons out there, and there were four American tanks taking on an enemy motorized rifle company, a reinforced motorized rifle company with 14 or 15 tanks. All this was within an eight-minute window, and still they were able to decimate that entire company.

"I think it goes back to the noncommissioned officers, the standards, the training level that we had reached at that point in our history as an army. There's no doubt that when we launched into Kuwait, we blew through not only the Iraqi Army but their Republican Guard, which were their best units. We went through them like water through a screen door."

— **Sergeant Major of the Army (ret) Kenneth O. Preston**
1st Sergeant, Alpha Company, 11th Cavalry, Operation Positive Force

Training Strategy

"When Mr. [Secretary of Defense] Cheney asked a soldier from the Spearhead Division if the enemy was tough, the young man replied: "Yes, Sir, they were pretty tough, but we fought a much tougher enemy in the Mojave Desert of California at the National Training Center!" To me, that vindicated what those of us who were part of the biggest revolution in the Army in my lifetime knew: that the war-fighting and training strategy of the U.S. Army at the NTC and other training centers was the most important and best strategy. That is really why the First Battle of Desert Storm was such an overwhelming victory."

— **Lieutenant General (ret) Paul "Butch" Funk**
Commander, 3rd Armored Division, Desert Storm

Only America

"Look at why America had to get involved in the fight. Here you had Saddam and the Iraqi Army that invaded Kuwait. Kuwait was an ally of ours. Naturally, Saudi Arabia to the south thought that Saddam might just continue moving even further south. I think it was important for us, because as I look at all the things that were going on in the world at that time, who else? Who else could have possibly intervened and stopped that? To take the fourth-largest army in the world and to knock them out of the top 10—I thought that was one of those feats that only America could have possibly done."

— **Sergeant Major of the Army (ret) Kenneth O. Preston**
1st Sergeant, Alpha Company, 11th Cavalry, Operation Positive Force 1991

sailors, and airmen were killed in action. The Coalition, by comparison, lost about 380 troops, including three U.S. female soldiers. Kuwaiti death figures vary, but approximately 1,000 Kuwaiti civilians were killed, and some 600 Kuwaiti military personnel are still listed as missing.

Superbly trained to a razor's edge of combat readiness, U.S. tankers consistently outgunned the Iraqis. Not only did the Americans have better, more modern and accurate equipment, they also had longer-range guns, superior navigational technology, and exceptional night-vision capabilities.

During much of those four days of fighting, the combatants also fought the weather—rain, blowing sand, and high winds. Fog, clouds, and smoke issued from the burning oil wells Saddam had blown up. While the smoke often obscured everyone's view, the Americans sported high-tech thermal sights, so the visibility wasn't nearly the problem for them as it was for the Iraqis.

Though the Republican Guard divisions outnumbered U.S. troops, the Americans' skill and aggressiveness, the quality of their training, the exceptional leadership, and the technical superiority all combined to give the Americans the advantage, and they quickly overwhelmed the Iraqis.

HOW WARS ARE WON

During the years that the United States rebuilt its military following the failures of the Vietnam Era, several key leaders in the U.S. military determined to rid themselves of the so-called "Vietnam syndrome." In tank warfare, and in all aspects of conducting a campaign, Americans determined to become skilled at asking themselves three essential questions: Where am I? Where are my friends? And where is the enemy?

Improvising Commanders

"Again, it goes back to confidence in your leaders. We want to develop confident, competent leaders because you can't be a confident leader if you're not competent, if you don't know your business. These commanders and these NCOs, they knew their business, and so you have to say they're going to make the right decision, and if they have to improvise they'll improvise—they did it magnificently. They improvised and solved the problem by the time we heard there was a problem.

"The one thing you learn—and this is a lesson from Vietnam—is you can't micromanage. Unfortunately, in Vietnam we had a lot of micromanagers, leaders who would get up in a helicopter and try to manage the war from 2,000 feet. You just can't do that. You've got to do your job ahead of time. We knew those division commanders, those corps commanders. We knew their staff guys. They had been with their units— they knew their men. And so we had confidence they were going to make the right decisions."

— **General (ret) Carl Vuono**
Chief of Staff, U.S. Army, Desert Storm

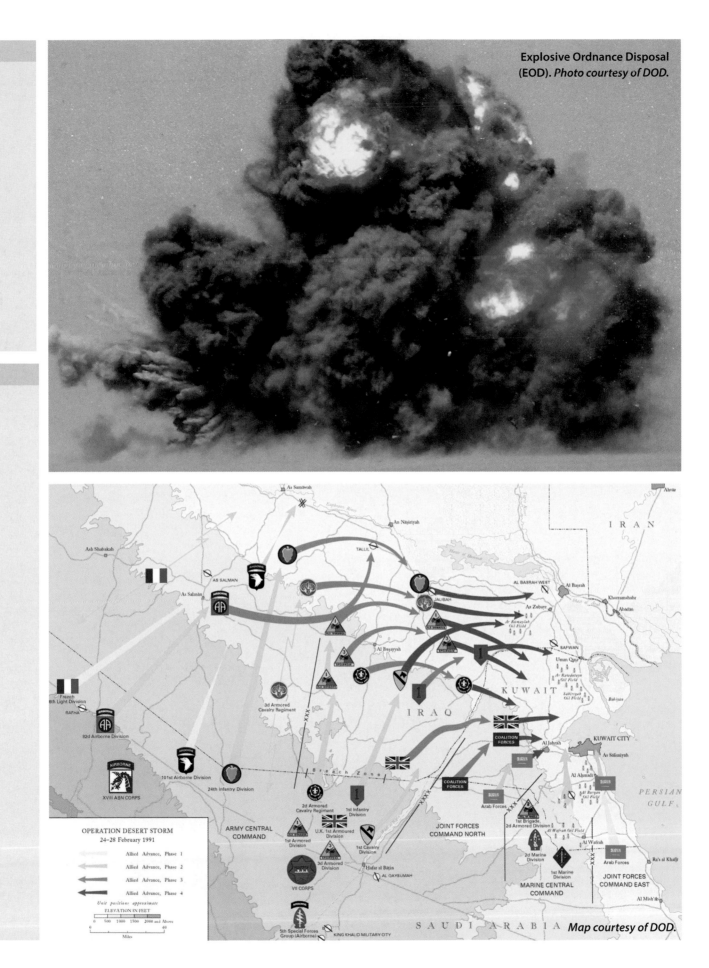

Explosive Ordnance Disposal (EOD). *Photo courtesy of DOD.*

Map courtesy of DOD.

OPERATION DESERT STORM
24–28 February 1991

Allied Advance, Phase 1
Allied Advance, Phase 2
Allied Advance, Phase 3
Allied Advance, Phase 4

Unit positions approximate

ELEVATION IN FEET

0   500 1000 1500 2000 and Above

0   40
Miles

Instant Thunder

"We put together a planning cell in the basement of the Pentagon, which came to be known as 'Checkmate.' That's where we began the original planning of what became the air campaign that we executed in Operation Desert Storm.

"That became the basis of an initial plan called 'Instant Thunder.' It was specifically designed and named to be the opposite of the Vietnam air war campaign known as 'Rolling Thunder.' We wanted to come down on Saddam's government and military like a thunderstorm, not a drizzle."

— Lieutenant General (ret) David Deptula
Principal attack planner, Desert Storm Coalition air campaign

"The idea behind Instant Thunder was to have a massive first-day attack against a whole set of targets. That attack would essentially blind and deafen Saddam so that he could neither receive reports from what was happening out in the Kuwait theater of operations nor do anything about it—because his command-and-control apparatus would be systematically dismantled on the first day."

— General (ret) Merrill "Tony" McPeak
Chief of Staff, U.S. Air Force (1990-94)

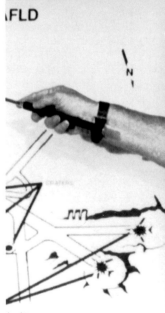

General Norman Schwarzkopf briefs press in Riyadh, Saudi Arabia. *Photo courtesy of NARA.*

An F-117S Nighthawk stealth fighter from the 37th Tactical Fighter Wing taxis into takeoff position. This aircraft made its debut during Operation Desert Storm. *Photo courtesy of NARA.*

A B-52G Stratofortress strategic bomber takes off on a mission during Operation Desert Storm. *Photo courtesy of NARA.*

Human Shields

"There was a time in which Saddam used human shields—Americans and British civilians who were basically detained and held at Iraqi strategic locations as a shield against any military action. Our embassy was almost in that category. At any moment it could be attacked—until Saddam Hussein in December 1990 finally decided that he was going to let all foreigners go, both from Kuwait and Iraq. It was a day-to-day situation.

"This was back in the days when long-distance calls had long-distance charges. I have often wondered what the State Department telephone bill was for calls to Baghdad and Kuwait that began on the first day of August and didn't end until mid-December. We were afraid if we dropped those lines, we'd never get them back, so we just kept them open the whole time."

— **Ambassador Ryan Crocker**, *U.S. Ambassador to Kuwait (1994-97)*

The U.S. Army adopted an ethos of being trained and ready to win the first battle of the next war.

This philosophy built the National Training Center in California, the Joint Readiness Training Center at Fort Polk, Louisiana, and the Joint Combat Maneuver Training Center at Hohenfels in Germany, as well as the Battle Command Training Program for senior-level commanders and units. It developed and fielded a Big Five collection of advanced technology weapons systems. All that enabled the U.S. Army, Air Force, Navy, and Marine Corps to train from individual trooper to senior leader to a razor-sharp edge of combat readiness.

In every after-action review of the war, service members and their leaders attributed their swift and decisive victory to the quality, skill, courage, and sacrifice of the U.S. troops, and their intense combined arms-training preparation and skill. This training had taken place in the U.S. military from the mid-1970s to Desert Storm, resulting in an overwhelming success rate in battle.

The U.S. military understood that through a new level of innovative training, and by using cutting-edge technologies, they could answer those three essential "where" questions with certainty every time. Through this enhanced new operational strategy and training, and learning from the mistakes of the Vietnam Era, military leaders would change the way warfare is conducted for all time.

This was the rethinking and retooling, the modernization that had started during the Reagan Administration and continued on through Desert Shield and Desert Storm. It was a revolution in modern warfare, because in the desert of Kuwait, under fire, the U.S. had technologies and equipment that told us precisely where we were and where our friends and enemies were, allowing our forces to do things on the battlefield that our rivals could not. ■

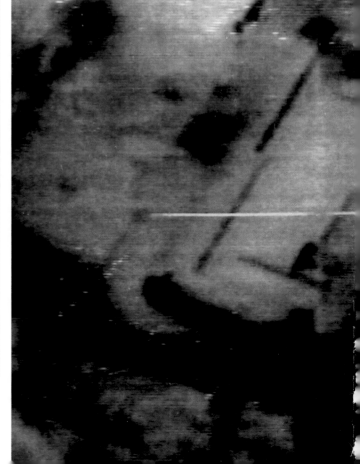

An AH-1W Sea Cobra from Marine Light Attack Helicopter Squadron 269 takes flight from USS *Nassau*. *Photo courtesy of NARA.*

An M1A1 Abrams main battle tank lays a smoke screen during maneuvers in Operation Desert Storm. *Photo courtesy of DOD.*

Tactical Surprise

"Surprise in war is rare, but we accomplished surprise at all three "Levels of War," in my opinion. Strategically, I don't think that hoodlum Hussein ever thought the president would commit U.S. Forces to the Middle East, and I am almost certain he never believed we would actually attack— particularly on the ground. Operationally, the Iraqi so-called "High Command" had no clue how quickly and competently the U.S. Army could re-position and attack over huge operational distances. Tactically, total surprise was confirmed when our 2nd Brigade interrogated a Republican Guards battalion commander they had captured at night. He said: 'Where did you guys come from? We thought you were at least 6 hours away!' That is tactical surprise of the first order."

— **Lieutenant General (ret) Paul "Butch" Funk**
Commander, 3rd Armored Division, Desert Storm

Desert Storm helicopter door gunner. *Photo courtesy of NARA.*

Televised Battle

"That famous night when we launched, everybody was watching it on television, listening to the reports coming in, and seeing these remarkable weapons that people had always wondered if they would work.

"Suddenly here come the Tomahawk missiles. I've often kidded that nobody thought we had weaponry like this, but then suddenly there's a Tomahawk missile flying down a street, waits for the red light to change, and then takes a right, and goes through the window of the building we were aiming for. Little bit of an overstatement, but it was that good.

"However, it caused me a problem by about Day Four because the media was starting to say, 'Well, why isn't this over already? Look at these things. Look at these weapons.' So Mr. Cheney and I had to go on television to calm people down. That's when I made an expression that became fairly well known: Our strategy is very simple. First we're going to cut them off, and then we're going to kill them. That kind of took the headline away, and everybody gave us time to work."

— **General Colin Powell,** *Chairman of the U.S. Joint Chiefs of Staff*

Targeting imagery from a USAF F-177 stealth fighter as it lines up for precision attacks on military targets in Iraq during Operation Desert Storm. *Photo courtesy of NARA.*

Turning Point in Modern Warfare

"Desert Storm was a turning point in the conduct of modern warfare. Because of the growth and maturity of technology, airmen were able to realize some of the theories that our aviation pioneers had posited since the 1920s and '30s.

"Remember, this was not a war against the people of Iraq. This was a war against Saddam Hussein and the military that had committed heinous aggression against Kuwait and its people. We weren't interested in a World War II-style war of attrition or an annihilation campaign against Iraqis.

"We wanted to minimize the impact on civilians and optimize our focus on getting Saddam to halt his aggression and remove himself from Kuwait. Which gets me to the second part of why this kind of air operation is critical: to minimize U.S. casualties.

"This was why the Desert Storm air campaign was such a turning point in the character of modern warfare. Any loss of innocent life is a bad thing. Before the war kicked off, General McCaffrey, who was a division commander at the time, testified in front of Congress that he anticipated there'd be a minimum of 10,000 casualties on the American side in the ground war. Well, there might have been if we had gone in with land forces upfront, but General Schwarzkopf was one of the first true joint-force commanders.

"While he was an Army general, he understood the value of using air power first. This was a 43-day air campaign. For the first 39 days, there were no boots on the ground. It was an all air-power show. He recognized that, and as a result of that sequencing of force and the parallel application of force across multiple centers of gravity across the breadth and depth of Iraq, our losses were very low.

"We were able to paralyze Saddam Hussein's ability to command and control his forces, causing them to collapse. That also resulted in reducing U.S. casualties. The entire operation—one that a renowned division commander estimated would cause 10,000 casualties—actually resulted in fewer than 150 Americans losing their lives. Of course, the precision weapons and tactics element played enormously into this outcome."

— Lieutenant General (ret) David Deptula
Principal attack planner, Desert Storm Coalition air campaign

Opposition to War

Even after the launch of Operation Desert Storm in January 1991, many from around the world—even in the Middle East and within the United States and Europe—continued to oppose using force to drive Saddam from Kuwait despite the depredations, rape, torture, and plunder Saddam's men carried out daily.

As the war began in earnest, a large anti-war demonstration took place in downtown Washington, D.C. Police estimated the number of participants at 75,000. However, all major polls of the American people showed solid support for President Bush's actions, with millions expressing their revulsion for the protesters' lack of support for the men and women in uniform who were risking their lives to liberate Kuwait.

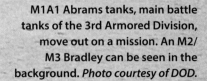

M1A1 Abrams tanks, main battle tanks of the 3rd Armored Division, move out on a mission. An M2/M3 Bradley can be seen in the background. *Photo courtesy of DOD.*

A Kuwaiti oil field set afire by retreating Iraqi troops burns in the distance beyond an abandoned Iraqi tank following Operation Desert Storm. *Photo courtesy of NARA.*

Activity hums around the San Diego-based amphibious assault ship USS *Tarawa* (LHA 1), as U.S. Marines go ashore in Kuwait. A Landing Craft Utility (LCU) leaves the ship's well deck with equipment and Marines from the 15th MEU (SOC), while a CH-53E Super Stallion helicopter heads to the beach. *Photo courtesy of DOD.*

U.S. Army UH-60A Black Hawk helicopters and one AH-64A Apache helicopter, second from right, conduct a mass takeoff during Operation Desert Storm. *Photo courtesy of NARA.*

Crew chief launches an F-16C Fighting Falcon aircraft during the first wave of the air attack in support of Operation Desert Storm. *Photo courtesy of NARA.*

A member of Marine Light Helicopter Squadron 767 (HML-767) fires an M2 .50 caliber machine gun from the door of a UH-1N Iroquois helicopter during Operation Desert Storm. *Photo courtesy of NARA.*

A Towering Victory

Initially intended to be a
telecommunications tower, the
structure was begun prior to
Saddam's invasion of Kuwait (see
image of tower under construction
on page 110) . To celebrate the
Kuwaiti victory and liberation from
Saddam's occupation, the building
was renamed the Liberation Tower.
It stands today as the second-tallest
structure in Kuwait. *Photo by Steve
and Jem Copley, licensed under
a Creative Commons Attribution-
NoDerivs 3.0 Unported License.*

Chapter 6
VICTORY

The feint was an amazing success. The U.S. ploy kept Saddam and his forces focused on Kuwait, eyes to the south, facing off against the U.S. Marines and Coalition forces moving methodically into Kuwait from Saudi Arabia. Then, when Saddam least expected, the VII Corps attacked out of the west desert, executing the surprise Left Hook and decimating the Iraqi Republican Guard divisions in southern Iraq.

Once the Coalition ground attack began in earnest, Iraq's occupiers in Kuwait quickly turned heel and fled north, hoping to reach the safety of Iraq. Life in Kuwait for Saddam's invaders was now lethal—their rape, pillage, and plunder of Kuwait would require a price.

THE HIGHWAY OF DEATH

On the night of February 27, 1991, Road 80—the main highway between Kuwait City and Basra, Iraq—became a most unhealthy commute. The Iraqi plunderers, many packed to the gunnels with loot they'd pillaged from Kuwaiti citizens, homes, and businesses, were now running for their lives. This was the same road so many of Saddam's forces had used the previous August to march arrogantly into a peaceful Kuwait. Now they fled in panic.

Actually, there were two "highways of death." The lesser known is Highway 8, located east of Road 80 and also running north to Basra. About 2,000 military and civilian vehicles were destroyed on Road 80, while perhaps another 300-400 vehicles were destroyed on Highway 8. Many Iraqis, mostly soldiers, lost their lives in these attacks—the official count varied wildly from 200 to 3,000.

RETRIBUTION

The images of the destruction along these highways are some of the most recognizable of the war. U.S. and Coalition warplanes rolled over the fleeing enemy with impunity, lighting up the desert horizon in a several-mile gauntlet of retribution. The absolute horror of being caught in such devastation resembled a scene from Dante's *Inferno* and was surely a night of living hell for Saddam's invaders.

Still, the carnage could have been far worse. When the Coalition bombed the leading Iraqi military vehicles and blocked the highways, the Iraqis piling up behind the disabled vehicles did not wait around—many fled into the desert. Soon after President Bush saw images of the ongoing destruction along these highways, and after consulting with General Schwarzkopf, he called CENTCOM for a cease-fire and ended the ordeal.

A formidable team had attacked Saddam's convoy: U.S. Marine A-6 Intruders, U.S. Air Force and Canadian Air Force fighters and bombers, and U.S. Navy jets from the aircraft carrier USS *Ranger* (CV 61). Adding insult to injury, those Iraqi soldiers who survived the pounding from the air were later engaged on the ground by arriving Coalition armor and mechanized infantry.

A few days later on Highway 8, General Barry McCaffrey's 24th Mechanized Infantry Division intercepted and wiped out elements of Al-Hammurabi, the Republican Guard 1st Armored Division, which was either attempting to escape or re-deploy.

Controversy has dogged these incidents ever since, with some commentators claiming that the Iraqis were in retreat and should not have been attacked so

ferociously. Others claimed that a number of civilians accompanied the fleeing army and should not have been subjected to such cruelty. General Schwarzkopf responded to the criticism:

> "The first reason we bombed the highway coming north out of Kuwait is because there was a great deal of military equipment on that highway, and I had given orders to all my commanders to destroy every piece of Iraqi equipment possible.
>
> "Second, this was not a bunch of innocent people just trying to make their way back across the border to Iraq. This was a bunch of rapists, murderers, and thugs who had raped and pillaged downtown Kuwait City and were now trying to get out of the country before they were caught."

ONE LAST SURPRISE FOR KUWAIT

On February 26, 1991, Iraqi troops began retreating from Kuwait en masse. The Coalition forces' advance into Kuwait proved more rapid than anyone anticipated. Though pockets of Iraqi resistance remained—most notably at the Kuwait International Airport—the Iraqi occupiers were done. Saddam, however, still had one last surprise for Kuwait.

In an act of vicious eco-terrorism, Saddam ordered his troops to set fire to 730 Kuwaiti oil wells and dump huge amounts of crude oil into Gulf waters. Coalition forces pursued the retreating troops to within 150 miles of Baghdad, and the Iraqis suffered considerable losses.

The Americans Are Coming

"Sheikh Ali was one of our leaders for the resistance. He called me and said, 'Ahmed, the Iraqis are under attack by the Coalition, led by America!' You cannot imagine the happiness we felt that night—we couldn't sleep, we were so happy! Everybody went to the roof and started shouting, 'Allah Akbar,' calling on God, thanking God. And on the other side, the Iraqis, they were worried.

"From that night onward, we were preparing ourselves for liberation day. 'Liberation day is coming!' we shouted.

"Our country was being bombed, but it's the first time we felt happy. Come on, America! In fact, any day that we didn't hear an airplane, we felt sad. 'Why don't they come?' we said. 'What's happened? Why don't they come?' My uncle would say, 'Ahmed, I wish President Reagan were here. Reagan would not wait like this.'

"I told him, 'Yes, President Bush is waiting too long!' Then he told me, 'Don't worry, Ahmad, just wait, see and learn. God bless his soul, President Bush. You just wait and see. It's not a matter of rushing. President Bush needs to make sure that they do it right.' And thank God, they did it absolutely right."

— **Ahmad Al-Rayyes,** *General Superintendent, Kuwait Oil Company*

A destroyed tank left behind by Saddam's forces against the backdrop of burning oil wells set ablaze by the retreating army. *Photo courtesy of Kuwait Ministry of Information.*

Real American Heroes

"The real hero of Desert Shield and Desert Storm is the American soldier. They didn't know exactly what they were getting into, they didn't know exactly what the war plan was until they crossed the line of departure, and yet they had great trust in their leaders. They were well trained, they were well equipped, and they had the technology that was necessary to succeed."

— **General (ret) Dennis Reimer**
U.S. Army Deputy Chief of Staff, Operations and Plans, Desert Storm

No Turning Back

"Soldiers of the Victory Division," said General Barry McCaffrey in his engagement orders, "we now begin a great battle to destroy an aggressor army and free two million Kuwaiti people. We will fight under the American flag and with the authority of the United Nations. By force of arms, we will make the Iraqi war machine surrender the country they hold prisoner. There will be no turning back when we attack into battle."

Iraqi military and civilian vehicles litter a section of a Kuwait Highway—nicknamed "The Highway of Death"—attacked by Coalition aircraft during Operation Desert Storm. *Photo courtesy of NARA.*

Abandoned tank stuck on Highway 80, between Basra and Kuwait. *Photo courtesy of Kuwait Ministry of Information.*

THE BEGINNING OF THE END

After the Iraqi Army was smashed in Kuwait and in full retreat, and several elite Republican Guard divisions were annihilated in southern Iraq, the Bush Administration began to discuss a possible cease-fire. After approximately 100 hours of lightning-fast ground war, and more than a month of U.S. and Coalition aircraft pounding the enemy from the air, Saddam's "fourth-largest army on earth" was near collapse.

After consulting with his Theater Commander, General Schwarzkopf, President Bush ordered a unilateral cease-fire effective February 28. On March 3, Coalition and Iraqi leaders met in Basra, which had been secured by the U.S. 1st Infantry Division, to discuss a formal cease-fire. After General Schwarzkopf met with Saddam's representatives and dictated the Iraqi terms of surrender, Iraq agreed to accept and follow all U.N. resolutions. The Coalition released its prisoners of war, and on April 6, 1991, Iraq signed a formal cease-fire agreement to terminate all hostilities.

By the time Operations Desert Storm and Desert Shield were over, more than 525,000 Americans had served in the fight. Nearly 300 Americans lost their lives in the war, about 150 in direct combat. Coalition combat deaths totaled around 300, and more than 450 Americans were wounded in action.

No one knows how many Iraqi military personnel served in the Kuwaiti theater of operations. Estimates are rough, ranging from 200,000 to well over 600,000. Approximate Iraqi deaths in combat were reported from between 10,000 to nearly 100,000.

WHAT DID THE WAR ACHIEVE?

Sometimes in the passion and celebration of victory, it is easy to forget the important lessons the war taught us—lessons from which we might benefit and for which we paid dearly.

Of course, the war achieved its original objective of driving Saddam's forces from Kuwait and doing so with minimal U.S. and Coalition losses. Such battlefield losses, in fact, were decisively one-sided. In addition, the Gulf War hammered out a new face of modern warfare. The war saw a modern leap in technology, not only in weapons development and usage but in intelligence coordination, in operational tactics, and in the incredible speed that leaders

The 100-Hour War

On February 28, approximately 100 hours into the ground war, President Bush declared a cease-fire. He spoke to the American people and the world:

"Kuwait is liberated. Iraq's army is defeated. Our military objectives are met. Kuwait is once again in the hands of Kuwaitis, in control of their own destiny. We share in their joy, a joy tempered only by our compassion for their ordeal.

"Tonight the Kuwaiti flag flies above the capital of a free and sovereign nation. And the American flag flies above our embassy. Seven months ago, America and the world drew a line in the sand. We declared that the aggression against Kuwait would not stand. And tonight, America and the world have kept their word."

— **President George H. W. Bush,** *February 28, 1991*

planned and executed air and armor operations. The technology helped keep the Iraqi enemy continually off-balance and confused.

New, sophisticated electronic warfare emerged along with precision strike capability that worked day or night and in all kinds of weather. Another hallmark of the war was the willingness and ability to coordinate a wide variety of military systems, cultures, languages, and political motivations that made up the Coalition. In the years following the Gulf War, the great military historian Sir John Keegan stated, "[The Gulf War] was a triumph of incisive planning and almost faultless execution."

On March 6, President Bush stood before the American Congress and announced that Kuwait was now liberated. The nation was free. Within days, American troops began to return home.

FAITH RESTORED

The Gulf War taught America much, mostly about herself. The war helped to once again endear and reunite the American people with their military. The war healed wounds that remained from the Vietnam debacle. It was gratifying, in fact, to see just how America had changed from the depressed, malaise-plagued period following the Vietnam War. Returning service members from the Gulf were welcomed as heroes throughout the country, with parades and speeches and great words of praise for their valiant service. The U.S. military once more became the respected icon it had been in years past. Faith in the capability and the honor of all branches of the U.S. Armed Forces was restored.

HOW THE GULF WAR CHANGED AMERICA AND THE WORLD

The Gulf War rushed upon the United States just as the Cold War was fading. With the world changing dramatically from two super-powers to numerous emerging, smaller power centers coming of age, people everywhere were seeking freedom and self-determination.

From this rapidly evolving environment emerged a tinhorn Middle East dictator who decided to grab something that was not his. Unfortunately for Saddam, he took on a military Lilliputian that happened to be a political, economic, and diplomatic giant. In essence, the Gulf War launched the United States into what President Bush called "a new world order."

From Germany to Arabia

"Probably one of the more interesting aspects, and one of the little-known accomplishments of Desert Storm, was the incredible move that had to take place to go from the southern part of Germany to the North Sea ports to deploy all that equipment. We had to move forces by air from the southern airfields in Germany and rendezvous in a desert in Saudi Arabia. It's an incredible story.

"In fact, I had a Russian general tell me later that the only military in the world that could have pulled that off was the U.S. military."

— **General (ret) Ronald Griffith**
Commander, 1st Armored Division, Desert Storm

Noncommissioned Officers

"Our success, as I see it, goes down to where the rubber meets the road, and that's with the noncommissioned officers out there who were the trainers, the subject-matter experts who were out there teaching those tank crews and instructing the soldiers in their roles and responsibilities."

— **Sergeant Major of the Army (ret) Kenneth O. Preston**
1st Sergeant, Alpha Company, 11th Cavalry, Operation Positive Force 1991

Driving Back to Kuwait

"I remember personally going into Kuwait three days after liberation. We traveled from Ta'if to the southern part of Kuwait and then drove in. It was the middle of the day, I remember, but it was like night because a big, dark cloud hung over Kuwait, and you could smell the burning oil. The smell in the air was unforgettable.

"The road was rough and full of debris, and we were zigzagging among destroyed vehicles and debris under the dark sky. We were in the middle of destruction, but we didn't care. We were happy to be back, no matter what.

"Within days, the government was operating, all the ministries were back and working, people were starting to get back to work. Everybody knew what they had to do. We stood back up on our feet very quickly."

— **Sheikh Salem Al-Sabah**
Kuwaiti Ambassador to the United States

Balanced Force

"I think the value of the Desert Shield/Desert Storm experience for America and our allies was that it was a very balanced force. When you think about the number of troops who were on the ground, Army and Marine Corps, the air forces that participated, the Navy that participated, it was really a joint operation that is a great model for the history books. In my mind's eye, the value of having boots on the ground is very important to this nation.

"What's the greatest commitment that the nation makes to any other country or to any other place? It's being willing to put their sons and daughters somewhere that they think is important. That commitment is very, very important to the strategy, to the operation, to the success."

— **General (ret) John H. Tilelli**
Commander, 1st Cavalry Division, Desert Storm

Coordinated Effort

"We saw in this conflict the electronic warfare domain that hadn't been around before—it was all being tried for the first time. The removal of Iraq from Kuwait was a result of a coordinated effort by air and ground forces, as well as sea and Navy forces from many different nations.

"We did have a sense that we were on a mission. It was truly a magnificent effort. I have a poster at home showing the Statue of Liberty rising from the waters with her torch of fire and the flags of all the countries that participated in that single effort to restore Kuwait to its rightful owners and to bring freedom back where it had been taken."

— **Rear Admiral (ret) Tom Marfiak**
Commander, Gulf Anti-Air Warfare, Desert Storm

U.S. pilot runs through flight preparations before refueling run. *Photo courtesy of NARA.*

Exit Strategy

"We went over there knowing that one thing Schwarzkopf had said, and I think Colin Powell said too, was, 'Hey, folks, this isn't Vietnam. We're going to go over, we're going to fight until it's concluded, then we're going to come home. We're not doing rotations, we're not moving out; that's not the plan. Don't expect it, so prepare to fight the long war, and when it's over you're coming home.' That's the mindset we had, and that's the mindset we kept. And when it ended, I was like, 'Holy cow, how did that happen? How did one hundred hours do the job?'"

— **Brigadier General Scott Morcomb**
224th Military Intelligence Battalion, Desert Storm

Two Seabees observe the surrounding area from a bunker during Operation Desert Storm. *Photo courtesy of NARA.*

Thirty-nine nations joined a coalition to liberate Kuwait. Since World War II, nothing on this scale had been seen before. The war was, for the first time, fought in real time, on television screens in living rooms around the world. Smart weapons, cruise missiles, and stealth bombers—new technologies that seemed fantastic and even surreal—amazed and sometimes confounded viewers. The new technology even transformed our vocabulary.

The world watched the ultimate reality TV show as the perfectly cast bad guy was demonized, then tricked like a fool, and finally smashed and humiliated and driven from Kuwait.

"OUR STRATEGY IS VERY SIMPLE"

In the process, with each "episode," a new cast of heroes emerged. There was General Schwarzkopf taking the battle to the enemy, then the Amir of Kuwait, protecting and inspiring his long-suffering people and winning the members of the United Nations to his cause.

President Bush played a starring role, forcefully stating to the world on primetime TV, "This will not stand, this aggression against Kuwait." General Colin Powell, Chairman of the U.S. Joint Chiefs of Staff, responded to queries about the attack. "Our strategy to defeat Saddam's army," he said, "is very, very simple: first we're going to cut it off, and then we're going to kill it."

In the end—which is really a new beginning—the Gulf War provided a sometimes frightening glimpse of what the new world would look like, where marvelous new technologies would empower both the good and the bad, both the great and the small, in ways few could yet envision. The Gulf War was an end *and* a beginning, displaying to the world the potential for peace, prosperity, and greatness, but also revealing a heightened danger the world had not yet seen.

The Gulf War marked a coming of age for the freedom-loving individual as well as the virulent, tyrant wannabe. Both extremes of good and bad see the new world of unimaginable opportunity and rapid change as a target-rich environment—one that could become either an earthly heaven or a deadly hell.

The war also demonstrated that with the right leadership, the future could well be bright with promise.

On February 28, President George H. W. Bush addressed the American people and the world:

"At every opportunity, I have said to the people of Iraq that our quarrel was not with them, but instead with their leadership and, above all, with Saddam Hussein. This remains the case. You, the people of Iraq, are not our enemy. We do not seek your destruction. We have treated your POWs

TV Coverage

"The significance of the liberation of Kuwait at the time was pretty great. First of all, it was a nonbelligerent country that had unfairly and in a devastating fashion been attacked. That the victory in Kuwait occurred showed that there are still forces of good in the world that would not let that happen.

"The other significance was, of course, the national interest of not only the United States but other countries around the world, and the region needed the stability that a victory would provide so that daily life—both individual life but also a nation's life—could be restored.

"But perhaps the most important new reality of the war was TV. The war, for the first time, saw real-time TV coverage of a variety of operations, thanks to reporters with cameras on the front lines, and even in the noses of smart bombs and missiles.

"As such, it was essential that the military work to control the message being fed to the American people and others. This was a war that the people of the world followed in real time in their living rooms. And the world has not been the same since."

— **Lieutenant General (ret) Roger Thompson**
Commander, 34th Transportation Group Europe, Desert Storm

The Crown Prince returns to Kuwait. *Photo courtesy of Kuwait Ministry of Information.*

An F-14A Tomcat from Fighter Squadron 41 (VF-41) banks into a turn while on a combat air patrol above Kuwait. *Photo courtesy of NARA.*

You Are All Heroes

Message from General Fred Franks to the VII Corps troops:

"We were ready. Our plan was to hit the enemy where he least expected and to press the attack in a short, violent air and ground fight of fire and maneuver throughout the depths of his formations.

"We did just that.

"You have my deepest admiration and thanks as your commander and as a fellow soldier. Our nations are grateful and thank you. Our Army is grateful and thanks you. You are victorious veterans of mobile armored desert warfare. You are the best we have. You have been great soldiers as demonstrated by your actions before the battle, your heroic performance during battle, and your magnificent humanitarian service after the battle. Your great versatility and sense of honor in battle and in humanitarian service are testament to who we are and what we stand for.

"I have been honored to be in your ranks and privileged to be given the responsibility to lead you into battle. You are all heroes and both our armies and our nations owe you everlasting thanks."

Deconfliction

"Imagine that you have two or three or four carriers launching aircraft. You also have Air Force aircraft up there. You have Marine Corps aircraft coming off the beach. You have allied aircraft flying out of Bahrain or Saudi Arabia.

"All these different types of aircraft have to be controlled, have to be maintained. You have to know where they are in space. They have to be able to get back to the right place without, in the process, misidentifying or perhaps shooting each other down. 'Deconfliction,' we called it: making sure that nobody gets the other guy's identification and position wrong.

"I'm very proud of the fact that we were able to do that over and over again. We did not have any blue-on-blue engagements throughout our tenure in the Gulf."

— **Rear Admiral (ret) Tom Marfiak**
Commander, Gulf Anti-Air Warfare, Desert Storm

with kindness. Coalition forces fought this war only as a last resort and look forward to the day when Iraq is led by people prepared to live in peace with their neighbors.

"This is not a time of euphoria, certainly not a time to gloat. But it is a time of pride: pride in our troops; pride in the friends who stood with us in the crisis; pride in our nation and the people whose strength and resolve made victory quick, decisive, and just. And soon we will open wide our arms to welcome back home to America our magnificent fighting forces.

"No one country can claim this victory as its own. It was not only a victory for Kuwait but a victory for all the Coalition partners. This is a victory for the United Nations, for all mankind, for the rule of law, and for what is right.

"This war is now behind us. Ahead of us is the difficult task of securing a potentially historic peace. Tonight though, let us be proud of what we have accomplished. Let us give thanks to those who risked their lives. Let us never forget those who gave their lives. May God bless our valiant military forces and their families, and let us all remember them in our prayers." ◼

Leadership

"As a young soldier, to hear the Commander in Chief, stand in front of the nation and really put his foot down and say, "This is what we're going to do," and then actually follow through with what he says we're going to do. That was empowering to me, to see that. I felt a lot of confidence in our leaders that even though there was a lot of uncertainty, I felt our leadership really supported us and had our backs."

— **Colonel Tyler Smith**
Specialist, 22nd Support Command, Desert Storm

Who Else?

"When you look at why America had to get involved into the fight, here you had Saddam and the Iraqi army that invaded Kuwait. It was an ally of ours. Who else could have possibly intervened and stopped that? That was one of those feats that only the American army could have possibly done."

— **Sergeant Major of the Army (ret) Kenneth O. Preston**
1st Sergeant, Alpha Company, 11th Cavalry, Operation Positive Force 1991

The Seven Essentials Learned from the Gulf War

1. Friends are worth fighting for

An old adage states, "Friends come and go, but enemies accumulate." Often those friends go because of neglect. The United States and her allied forces learned from the Gulf War that friends can save your life and can come to your aid, bringing invaluable skills and resources. But mostly, they saw what happens when, like Saddam Hussein, you have no friends at all. In the end, not even terrorist groups for whom he had provided safe haven would offer him a hand.

2. The power of the honorable victory

Victory, honor, and strength are, without a doubt, essential qualities in the Middle East. People naturally gravitate toward the strong horse and away from the weak one. When America appears to the world as weak, indecisive, and in decline, its honor and respect craters, signaling to friends and enemies that the country is vulnerable. Honor and shame are opposite ends of the survival spectrum in the Middle East. Perhaps the least-understood element of U.S. foreign policy is how to successfully enhance America's honor without bringing her shame.

3. The United States can't ignore the Middle East

The Middle East is the fulcrum, the essential connector between Asia, Europe, and Africa. It is key to America's prosperity and security. Its importance stems from economics, politics, religion, demographics, and the tsunami of modern technologies sweeping the globe, especially information technologies and weapons technologies. The Middle East comprises half a billion young, dynamic, motivated Muslim youth coming of age in the Middle East and Muslim world who will either be a force for peace and prosperity or become enemies of the free world. In sum, the United States does not have the luxury of ignoring the Middle East. Today more than ever, the Middle East matters.

4. The Middle East is unpredictable

Nothing regarding the Middle East is set in stone, regardless of the traditional belief of predestination. The Middle East cultural concept of "Leave it to God" cannot be the basis of U.S. regional policy. Yes, the place is unpredictable and even explosive, but the Gulf War taught the United States that skilled diplomacy—along with effective political and military planning with the right friends—can change the world for the better. The liberation of Kuwait showed that the future is not set in stone.

5. Success in the Middle East will depend upon the successful union of politics and war

War is politics, as the military historian Carl von Clausewitz so famously noted. But it's a most delicate, even dangerous, balance. The Gulf War showed how to balance both to accomplish a just and rewarding end. Such an approach is never easy. But it can be done—and done well—with the right dedication, the right diplomatic and military skill and preparation, and most importantly, the will.

6. Skilled leaders are indispensible

History is made by the skilled choices of great men and women. The Gulf War demonstrated how essential respected leadership is to peace, freedom, and prosperity. Remove Bush, Cheney, Baker, Powell, and Schwarzkopf from this story, and the outcome might have been entirely different. Considering the opposition to war from powerful people at the time, Saddam very likely would not have been removed from Kuwait. As such, many lives today would be much different—less secure, less prosperous—with Saddam and his psychotic sons destabilizing the region. Leadership matters, and quality leadership is hard to come by. The Gulf War helped the world see why.

7. In the end, there is no other choice

In his famous "Give Me Liberty or Give Me Death" speech, Patrick Henry proclaimed, "We have no choice, if we were base enough to desire it. It is now too late to retire from the contest. There is no retreat but in submission and slavery!"

While some might brand this refusal to retreat as alarmist rhetoric, history shows otherwise. The Middle East and the United States, if not the entire world, are now increasingly locked in an ever-accelerating, ever-dangerous downward spiral. But with the right leadership cultivating useful and valuable alliances between nations, the Middle East has the potential of inspiring a new age of prosperity and freedom linking a cooperative Europe, Asia, and Africa to create a new renaissance. The choices of great men and women make history and shape the future—the Gulf War proved that in spades.

A 401st Tactical Fighter Wing F-16C Fighting Falcon aircraft prepares to take off. *Photo courtesy of DOD.*

Kuwaitis celebrate liberation. *Photo courtesy of Kuwait Ministry of Information.*

Kuwaitis celebrate liberation. *Photo courtesy of Kuwait Ministry of Information.*

American Readiness

"It's something that we can reflect back in our history and be proud of all the training, the readiness, the preparation and it's not just the army. It's the American people. It's their investment. It's the taxpayer dollars that go into being able to maintain and upkeep an army that's ready when the nation calls."

— **Sergeant Major of the Army (ret) Kenneth O. Preston**
1st Sergeant, Alpha Company, 11th Cavalry, Operation Positive Force 1991

Grateful Kuwaitis

"I don't think Americans know the depth of the appreciation that Kuwaitis still have for what the United States and other Coalition partners did in liberating their country. I remember a little more than a year ago when I was in a shopping mall here [in Kuwait], a stranger came up to me, shook my hand, and said, 'I want to thank you for what the United States did for Kuwait.'

"I smiled and then walked on. I said to myself, 'That's interesting.' But what I've found over the past 15 months is that it has happened over and over, on street corners, at receptions, in shopping malls."

— **Ambassador Douglas Silliman**
U.S. Ambassador to Kuwait (2014 - Present)

General Norman Schwarzkopf, Commander, CENTCOM, Operation Desert Storm. *Photo courtesy of NARA.*

A CH-53E Super Stallion helicopter idles on the flight deck of aircraft carrier USS *Saratoga* (CV 60). *Photo courtesy of NARA.*

Joint Force Commander

"General Schwarzkopf really was the epitome of a joint-force commander. He didn't get into details; what he did was provide guidance. He listened to his component commanders. This was the first major use of force after the landmark Goldwater–Nichols Legislation of 1986, which introduced a 'joint perspective' to the conduct of warfare.

"This is enormously significant and reflective of the differences in the way the services operated post Goldwater–Nichols. The bottom line as a result of this legislation is that the services now closely coordinated their activities. The Army, Navy, Air Force and Marine Corps organized, trained, and equipped together as service components to provide forces through a joint task force commander—in this case, General Schwarzkopf. The Joint Task Force would then assign and organize all components to meet the needs of a particular contingency.

"The new organizational scheme was something called Functional Component Commander—instead of Army, Navy, Air Force, and Marines each employing their different aviation assets in their own way. The joint force air component commander was the one responsible for integrating all these assets into one highly focused force.

"That's what General Horner did. He was Joint Force Air Component Commander. I was his offensive air campaign planner who wrote the attack plans for each and every day of the war against Iraq. As part of the planning, I didn't care what service or what country was painted on the side of an airplane. What I cared about was what kind of capability each airplane had.

"General Schwarzkopf was truly the epitome of a joint force commander because he didn't think just as an Army four-star general. He thought about the best ways to use the capabilities provided by airmen, soldiers, sailors, and marines to meet the needs of our overarching joint operation."

— **Lieutenant General (ret) David Deptula**
Principal attack planner, Desert Storm Coalition air campaign

Kuwaiti oil fields set on fire by
Saddam's retreating forces.
Photo courtesy of Kuwait
Ministry of Information.

Damage done by Saddam's army to Kuwaiti cities and infrastructure was extensive. The Telecommunications Tower stands partially built in the background. This tower was later renamed the Liberation Tower when it was completed after the Gulf War. *Photo courtesy of Kuwait Ministry of Information.*

Chapter 7
THE DEVASTATION OF KUWAIT

Saddam was a sore loser. If he couldn't have the production of hundreds of Kuwaiti oil wells, nobody would. If he couldn't outright own Iraq's 19th Province, he'd leave it in shambles. On January 22, 1991, he instructed his men to begin detonating pre-set charges on Kuwait's many oil rigs and wells. In short order, more than 700 wellheads were destroyed and burning, belching a curtain of black smoke that could easily be seen from earth-orbiting satellites or the Space Shuttle, instigating the world's worst man-caused environmental disaster in history.

SADDAM, THE VINDICTIVE

The destruction of Kuwait was a contingency of Saddam's master plan. As the Coalition steadily amassed troops in Saudi Arabia, and the United Nations continued to get behind Kuwait and its friends and allies, Saddam began to see that keeping Kuwait was increasingly unlikely. So he stepped up his plan to punish the state and to shame the Kuwaitis before the world.

Amazingly, satellite imagery began to provide evidence that Saddam was building a pipeline from a major Kuwaiti oil field to Arabian Gulf waters. According to reports smuggled out from the Kuwaiti resistance, Saddam planned to dump millions of barrels of oil into Gulf waters if the Coalition attacked him, fouling Kuwait's water desalinization plants, pristine beaches, and fishing grounds—setting the oil ablaze was even a possibility. Saddam knew this would cause damage to the Saudis as well as other Gulf emirates, but the consequences were irrelevant. He would have Kuwait intact, or nobody would.

PLUNDER

The Iraqis came to plunder. This was not just an invasion of a friendly, peaceful neighbor to "teach a lesson," as some world leaders claimed. This was a carefully planned and organized raid, bent on long-term occupation and systematic rape and ransack.

As soon as the Iraqis had secured Kuwait, Saddam's troops began stripping valuables from Kuwait's hospitals, banks, TV and radio stations, stores, factories, government buildings, schools and universities, hotels, and even fast-food restaurants. They used stolen Kuwaiti trucks to haul the loot out. Even the animals in Kuwait's zoo were shot, released, or left to starve. The Iraqi invasion became one mammoth and messy salvage operation. And what the raiders couldn't steal, they smashed, burned, or blew up.

COMMON BRUTALITIES

Jacques, a Lebanese expatriate working in Kuwait, had a fine job working with a branch of the Al-Sabah family during the occupation. His two teenage sons had gone to school with a number of Kuwaiti youth, and hung out with them on occasion. When the invasion took place, the Iraqi Mukhabarat came to Jacques' apartment and arrested one of his sons, claiming that he was assisting the Kuwaiti resistance.

The teenage boy was taken to a torture and interrogation center and brutalized over the next several weeks. Desperate, Jacques attempted to gain his son's release by bringing cash and valuables to his son's captors—anything that might persuade the police to free him. But instead of softening or releasing the boy, the Iraqi police cruelly assaulted the grieving father.

Jacques, who had heart problems to begin with, suffered a massive heart attack and died. The Mukhabarat threw his body in a car and dumped him on the doorstep of his apartment for his wife to find. The family was forced to bury Jacques in an unmarked grave. It was not until after Kuwait's liberation that the family was able to place a gravestone on his final resting place. Eventually, the Iraqis released the teenage son after weeks of torture.

THE MERCIES OF THE MERCILESS

Such stories were hardly unique during the occupation. From His Highness the Amir and his honored brother, Sheikh Fahd, who was shot by the invaders while defending his family, to thousands of Kuwaitis and expatriates such as Jacques, all were subjected to brutalities that became far too commonplace. In such an environment, forced to rely on the mercies of the merciless, human life in occupied Kuwait became dirt cheap.

The Iraqis placed countless mines in the sand along the seaside, making the beaches absolutely lethal to visit. Steel spikes, barbed wire, and machine-gun bunkers were scattered along the seafront road. Bunkers were built high in apartments and hotels facing the Bay and Gulf waters, perches for Iraqi snipers, machine gunners, and spotters.

Minefields and Oil

"There were 730 wells on fire on all major oil fields in Kuwait and around 400 wells gushing. The oil flowed under very high pressure. Because of the velocity of the flow, it sucked deep groundwater up the hole, mixing with the oil, which made it difficult for the well to be ignited. So, it gushed oil out onto the field, which we had to work around to reach those burning wells. That was a major obstruction for us.

"Also, the oil field was [booby-trapped] with cluster bombs and mines that the Iraqis placed. We found very long minefields set by the Iraqis. We had to deal with the mines, so we hired expert companies to work with us. I formed around 16 teams to go out daily to clear the way. That was a major task."

— **Saud Al-Nashmi**
Drilling Operations Manager, Kuwait Oil Company

Pipelines to Pollute the Gulf

"We received intelligence from Kuwaiti resistance working as engineers in Kuwait Oil Company [under Iraqi occupation], information that the Iraqis were laying two major pipelines from the northern fields to the Arabian Gulf.

"Their plan was to open up the oil fields and dump crude in the water of the Gulf, choking Kuwait water distillation plants and maybe other areas, including Saudi Arabia and the rest of the Gulf states. So, the Pentagon was seriously watching this as a main priority, and I was there to help explain how the Iraqis would send the flow from the northern fields to Gulf waters. That was very important at the time. We could watch them through the satellites. We could see the new pipelines."

— **Saud Al-Nashmi**
Drilling Operations Manager, Kuwait Oil Company

Looting Kuwait

"I had a friend who told me this story: he was in his house when the Iraqis came to get him. So he dressed himself as a servant and said, 'I'm sorry, but the master is not here.'

"He then closed the front door, went out the back door, and made it to Saudi Arabia to safety. For the Kuwaitis caught inside, it was not something you saw on CNN; it was not something that appeared on a remote broadcast someplace; it was up close and personal.

"It was interesting, however, that the Iraqis returned and went into his house and took everything out down to the bare walls, including the fixtures from the bathrooms and so on. Just ripped them right out of his place. Finally, there was nothing left, it was just a shell. And that was not a unique experience, by any means."

— **Rear Admiral (ret) Tom Marfiak**
Commander, Gulf Anti-Air Warfare, Desert Storm

Blazing oil wells, damaged pipelines and other industry infrastructure caused by Saddam's forces required Kuwaitis to act quickly to bring their oil production back online. *Photo courtesy of Kuwait Ministry of Information.*

Small and large businesses were left devastated by the war. *Photo courtesy of Kuwait Ministry of Information.*

Many American and British fast-food franchises were not only stripped to the paint by the occupiers, but blown up and burned just for spite. Five-star hotels were gutted, room after room emptied of furnishings and fixtures of all kinds. Schools and hospitals were stripped to the walls. Expensive roofing systems were torn from their structures, and thousands of cars stolen from private citizens and car dealers, then driven or shipped to Iraq. Even such random items as street lamps, front doors of houses, and children's swings and slides caught the fancy of these unwelcome guests.

At the base of the iconic Kuwait Towers along the seafront, Iraqi soldiers fired rocket-propelled grenades into the concrete bases, hoping to do enough damage to topple the towers. However, the concrete was so thick and the reinforced steel around that massive foundational base so strong that the rockets barely made divots in the surface.

THE MOSQUE: THE ONLY SAFE GATHERING PLACE

Since so many of the normal places of social gathering (malls, restaurants, parks, the zoo, etc.) were now destroyed or off-limits, Kuwaitis found solace and a place to maintain social connections in the nation's many mosques. There they could meet with family and friends and even, if they were discreet, discuss the occupation and how best to survive and resist it.

Public gatherings were prohibited anywhere else, so Friday worship meetings provided excellent cover for not only learning who was doing what, but also for coordinating how best to attack the occupiers. The meetings also provided the perfect place for conversations about how and where to get needed food, medicine, and other necessities which were becoming increasingly difficult to find.

AVOIDING FURTHER LOSSES IN KUWAIT

It was not long before parts of Kuwait took on the look of a post-apocalyptic film set—especially after the wellheads were set on fire. Other areas, though, appeared relatively unscathed. The Iraqis could be thorough under certain circumstances, but their demolition was inconsistent throughout Kuwait.

As Americans and the Coalition planned the liberation, they tried hard to avoid making Kuwait a battleground, which would only further destroy what remained. The feint from the south and from the sea, along with the subsequent Left Hook through the west desert, were designed not only to quickly overwhelm the Iraqi invaders but also to draw the tens of thousands of occupiers out of Kuwait back into Iraq and engage them there.

Carefully planned and successfully executed through this tactic, the Bush Administration and the Coalition helped to preserve what was left of the infrastructure of the State of Kuwait and protect those Kuwaitis and other civilians still under occupation. Under the circumstances, it was a most humane battle plan.

With the Iraqis fleeing Kuwait, the massive reconstruction of the country began. The first requirement, of course, was to feed and care for the people, particularly the infirm and the aged, who were now emerging from basements, damaged homes, and other hiding places. Medical provisions were provided right away, and food was shipped to multiple outlets. Government ministries began to re-staff and provide crucial services. But the most pressing national effort was to extinguish the hundreds of well fires and cap the wells and pipelines gushing crude oil.

THIRD ARMY LAUNCHES TASK FORCE FREEDOM

Third Army Commander Lieutenant General John Yeosock sent in Task Force Freedom—commanded by Major General Robert Frix and his deputy Brigadier General Howard Mooney, Commander of 352nd Civil Affairs Brigade—to Kuwait City with the mission of aiding Kuwait in its recovery. They went to work immediately, even before the formal cease-fire went into effect on March 1, 1991, and continued until April 15, when the mission was turned over to the U.S. Army Corps of Engineers. Under President Bush's direction, Task Force Freedom was formed in coordination with CENTCOM and the Kuwaiti government in exile. President Bush was determined to restore the legitimate government of Kuwait and assist in ensuring that its citizens could reinhabit the country as soon as possible.

General Colin Powell, Chairman of the U.S. Joint Chiefs of Staff, gave the following speech to our troops at the end of the war:

> "Thank you for your magnificent victory in the Gulf, and I also want to say thank you on behalf of the liberated people of Kuwait and others in the Arabian Gulf region whose security you have ensured by your gallantry in action. . . . You have raised the levels of warfare to new heights. You fought a war of complexity and integration that no one has ever seen before. You were at the top of the profession of arms. . . . You have made America proud again. You have made America feel good about herself again. You have made America realize that there is nothing we can't do if we put our hearts to it, if we put our minds to it, and if we put our muscles to the task before us." ■

Online in Seven Months

"I headed up 16 teams of mine-clearance specialists, as well as 27 well-control teams. All were led by managers and team leaders who carried out our plan, which spelled out which wells we would like to cap first. From the early days, we identified certain wells from the Ahmadi Field that were gushing oil and gas and smoke over and around the town of Ahmadi and over the hospital. We controlled these wells first, at the beginning of our task, and then we moved to the more difficult and less accessible wells around the field.

"It was really a surprise to many nations in the region, because much smoke covered their countries, and they thought that Kuwait would not get back online until likely several years. But to the surprise of the whole world, we accomplished a miracle on the ground, by the help of God and the strength of our rulers and Kuwaiti people who supported us all the way.

"We also thank our resistance inside Kuwait who demonstrated a marvelous, courageous support for us and to defend our country. The whole effort brought Kuwait's oil industry back from destruction in only seven months!"

— **Saud Al-Nashmi**
Drilling Operations Manager, Kuwait Oil Company

Many buildings were littered with debris and left unstable by bomb blasts. *Photo courtesy of Kuwait Ministry of Information.*

Al Watanlya Souk

Landmines were often used by Saddam's forces around burning oil fields. *Photo courtesy of Kuwait Ministry of Information.*

Many businesses, palaces, and mosques were left in ruin by Saddam's invading army. *Photo courtesy of Kuwait Ministry of Information.*

The war-torn landscape of Kuwait heading north to Iraq was littered with many damaged and burned-out vehicles. Coalition troops often spray-painted graffiti on the abandoned vehicles as they pushed Saddam's troops northward. *Photo courtesy of Kuwait Ministry of Information.*

العبدلي
Abdaly
75 KM   ٧٥ كم

B co 143RD SIGNAL

K.C. WAs HeRe

His Highness the Amir of Kuwait, Sheikh Jaber Al-Ahmad Al -Jaber Al-Sabah, returns to Kuwait to help in the rebuilding process. *Photo courtesy of Kuwait Ministry of Information.*

Chapter 8

KUWAIT RISING: REBIRTH AND REBUILDING

The Kuwaiti government in exile had no illusions. Its nation had been violated and spoiled, its people brutalized. Saddam had done his level best to erase or at least steal and destroy the free and prosperous State of Kuwait. But now that Kuwait was finally free of the invader, a new and challenging task—the next chapter in the story—lay ahead.

With the renowned Kuwaiti oil industry in ruins and on fire, the government once again turned to its friends and partners. Specialists of all stripes gathered from every corner of the globe to lend a hand. The United States possessed the finest, most experienced oil-well firefighters in the world, so they came. Some, such as Red Adair, were walking legends.

Countries from around the world sent in teams to tackle this dirty and dangerous task. After eight months, a team of skilled Hungarian engineers came up with the idea of mounting a Russian MiG jet engine on a trailer, rolling the engine up to a burning well, and firing up the jet—literally blowing the inferno out.

THE FORLORN LAND

Still, the gigantic task of dealing with more than 700 burning and gushing wells seemed daunting to most and impossible to some. Not only were the flaming wells deadly to approach because of the heat, but the ground surrounding the wells was an oily quagmire of spilled petroleum mixed with powdery dust and dirt.

Even worse, the fleeing Iraqi soldiers had set hundreds of mines and cluster bombs around many of the wells to kill and maim anyone attempting to cap them. To the many armchair "experts," saving the wells appeared out of the question. Meanwhile, black, belching smoke had turned Kuwait into a dark and hellish, hopelessly grimy and depressing land, with oily smoke coating everything. Even the sun fled this forlorn land, blocked from the sky by the billowing, coal-black clouds spreading across the horizon.

REBIRTH

Incredibly, however, as the armed forces of the Coalition departed, a new international army arrived with men and women who had expunged the word "can't" from their vocabulary. With courage and skill, this rare breed of professionals showed the world in just eight months how to extinguish the impossible, then cap the gushing wells and begin the clean-up of a nation barely emerging from occupation and war.

The rebirth and rejuvenation of Kuwait became yet another miracle of the 20th century, as the world watched a small nation prove it could come back from devastation stronger than ever.

THE U.S. MILITARY: FIRST IN WAR, FIRST IN PEACE

The VII Corps was the last unit out of Iraq, based on the theater policy of "first in, first out." For the better part of seven weeks—until the United Nations gave the order to withdraw on April 13, 1991—VII Corps and an attached French company conducted humanitarian operations.

VII Corps units also continued to destroy captured Iraqi equipment and ammunition. VII Corps assisted the resettlement of refugees, including more than a thousand Kuwaiti citizens held against their will in Iraq. With the permission of the Saudi Government, VII Corps engineer units built a refugee camp in Saudi Arabia where almost 20,000 war refugees were moved to await resettlement. More than 8,000 of those refugees came by C-130 USAF transports from Safwan, Iraq. U.S. Army doctors, physician assistants, nurses, and medics treated close to 30,000 patients, some of whom were evacuated to hospitals in Saudi Arabia for further treatment.

VII Corps units distributed more than 1.5 million gallons of water and more than one million meals, in addition to providing staples such as rice, flour, and beans. Other humanitarian operations went on throughout the area as schools reopened and areas cleared of munitions. The very same soldiers who weeks before had attacked and destroyed Iraqi units now provided for the needs of thousands of war refugees. Such was the legacy of those who fought to resist tyranny and to protect the innocent. Such was the legacy of the veterans of Desert Storm.

AN OPEN-DOOR POLICY TO THE WORLD

The quick transition from war to peace was incredible to witness on every front. Prior to the invasion and occupation, Kuwait was a land with only a marginal desire to open its doors to the influences of other nations and cultures. But after Kuwait was liberated, the country extended a firm hand of friendship to many lands and nationalities, particularly to the United States.

In true Arab fashion, Kuwait refused to forget its friends and, even more so, embraced progress and enlightenment. The war had taught Kuwait that its power lay in its ability to use refined diplomatic skills and organizational prowess, to embrace the good abroad, and to take advantage of opportunities.

TINKER, TAILOR, SOLDIER, SPY

The American service member comes in many uniforms, including no uniform at all, representing a broad spectrum of service-oriented entities—some absolutely visible, and some never seen. Those who arrived in the Middle East in 1990 and 1991, along with those already there, combined to

Pride in Service and Country

"As I like to tell the Kuwaitis, there were about 700,000 American Soldiers, Sailors, Airmen, Marines, and Coast Guard members who were deployed for the operation to liberate Kuwait. That means 700,000 mothers, 700,000 fathers, millions of spouses and children and brothers and sisters, and tens of millions of neighbors, friends, and extended family who were watching the news very closely, like my family was, and praying for the safe return of their loved ones who had been deployed for Operation Desert Storm and Operation Desert Shield.

"By the time of Operation Desert Storm, I think people fully appreciated what the impact was on the soldiers and their families. Even before the end of the successful operation, you saw yellow ribbons and American flags and Kuwaiti flags appearing everywhere, as well as 'Free Kuwait' bumper stickers, and 'Free Kuwait' posters and billboards.

"There was an amazing confluence of our desire to help Kuwait and make it free with our desire to support the American men and women who had gone to help liberate Kuwait and protect the rest of the Gulf. It was the pride in the military, the pride in the service of our countrymen, that really struck me throughout the campaign, but especially after the successful completion."

— **Ambassador Douglas Silliman**
U.S. Ambassador to Kuwait (2014 - Present)

Graffiti-covered wall in the wake of Saddam's destruction. *Photo courtesy of Kuwait Ministry of Information.*

Oil well fires rage outside Kuwait City in the aftermath of Operation Desert Storm. The wells were set on fire by Iraqi forces before they were ousted from the region by Coalition forces. *Photo courtesy of DOD.*

Rubble left by Saddam's fleeing army.
Photo courtesy of NARA.

comprise a powerful coalition of the willing.

They were not there to pillage or to plunder. They were not there to occupy and keep another's land or personal property. They were there to train, plan, and prepare, then finish their work and go home. Such has always been the way of American servicemen and women.

MAGNIFYING THE POWER OF LIBERATION

In the same vein, the State of Kuwait sees itself as a nation preserved in war to become an economic engine to bless not only its own people, but hardworking people from scores of other lands. Honest and dedicated people from poor nations have opportunities in Kuwait they would not have had in their home countries.

In Kuwait, these immigrants know toil and loyalty will pay great dividends, and their opportunities will be magnified depending upon their own willingness to work and serve. Then, with money in hand, they send home remittances that not only bless their families but also raise the standard of living of their homelands.

The liberators of Kuwait, the Coalition veterans, need to know that their sacrifices have been multiplied many times, blessing millions more than just the ones they originally fought to free. This is the power of liberation in a globalized world, the multiplying effect on countless others when freeing a generous and giving people, a nation such as Kuwait.

The liberators of Kuwait have proven to the world, and to dictators and tyrants everywhere, the power of freedom and what free people and nations can accomplish when given the chance and when inspired by skilled, dedicated, self-sacrificing leaders.

Kuwaiti Children

"At the end, it was wonderful to be able to see the smiles, the kids, the families. The kids—that was amazing. They would come up and give us hugs, always give us their time, thanking us on behalf of their families as we came back into the country, as we were redeploying after Kuwait was liberated. This monster, Saddam Hussein, was gone. We recognized that the people of Kuwait were most generous and most thankful to the American soldiers.

"In fact, later I went back to Kuwait as part of my job. I told the young officer who was checking my passport that I was back in Kuwait and that I was here in 1991. He thanked me, stood up, and gave me a hug. So it was nice. They didn't forget. They recognized what we did and recognized our true partnership with the Kuwaitis, even now."

— **Lieutenant Colonel (ret) Scott Rutter**
Commander, C Company, 2-16 Infantry,
1st Infantry Division, Desert Storm

In other words, it does matter who controls key real estate. Unlike the Saddam Husseins of the world, wise leadership takes a nation's resources and shares it with others—not just its own citizens. Such a wise, strategic move magnifies an existing capital base and multiplies the power of a nation's resources many times over, blessing millions.

In addition, capable leaders see the strength that education and individual entrepreneurial accomplishment bring to their nations. Every year, Kuwait sends more than 10,000 students to study and achieve in the United States.

Kuwait's positive impact and influence in the world goes far beyond what a small city-state would normally contribute. This magnifying effect comes from a combination of skilled management, education, and training opportunities, and the use of capable and effective diplomatic outreach. One look at Kuwait's rising city skyline today and the observant will understand that Kuwait's future success and true potential are yet to be realized—what is happening now is just the beginning.

ACHIEVING SUCCESS

No nation or people have yet found a workable formula for economic and social utopia. But Kuwait has become the land of opportunity for many, a land rising in the world and proving to all nations what freedom and its accompanying benefits can accomplish for the common man and woman willing to work. Kuwait is special because the country and its leaders understand the advantages to all of helping those less fortunate to also achieve their own success.

KUWAIT RISING

Today, Kuwait produces one of the world's strongest economies with one of the highest GDPs per capita. Kuwait is perhaps the most engaged nation in the Gulf Cooperation Council, an organization of nations including Saudi Arabia, Bahrain, Qatar, the UAE, and Oman. Kuwait's citizens are open and receptive toward their neighbors and maintain an active and domestically powerful parliament.

In May 2005, Kuwaiti women received the right to vote. Since then, women have been elected to the Kuwaiti

The Embassy's American Flag

"After the invasion and liberation, Nathaniel Howell, the U.S. Ambassador to Kuwait, had one of the best jobs in the world because he was Mr. Popularity. So many Kuwaitis would talk with gratitude for what the U.S. had done for them, the sacrifices we made, the American lives we lost to liberate their country. For those who rode out the occupation, they said repeatedly they just had to look out and see that the American flag was still there, kind of like our national anthem.

"Interesting footnote to that—once the invasion had begun, embassy personnel went through their store rooms to find the biggest flag they had to run up the pole, to show Kuwaitis and Iraqis that America was still there.

"The embassy finally evacuated in December 1990 when Saddam agreed that all Americans could get out. We were the last embassy left open. Ambassador Howell left the flag up, and word soon spread by that wonderful Kuwaiti resistance, 'Boy, listen, the Americans have mined that compound up, down, back, forward, left, right, so if anybody goes through that gate, it's going to be Hiroshima for sure!'

"So, for whatever reason, even after we were gone, the Iraqis never entered the embassy compound. That flag flew from the day of occupation to the day of liberation, unmolested."

— **Ambassador Ryan Crocker**
U.S. Ambassador to Kuwait (1994-97)

In the aftermath of the war, many Kuwaitis found their belongings destroyed or looted. *Photo courtesy of Kuwait Ministry of Information.*

Saddam's army looted the property of many Kuwaiti citizens. *Photo courtesy of Kuwait Ministry of Information.*

Working Together

"After liberation, there was a sense of camaraderie, a sense of working together, the energy, just the excitement of trying to rebuild and to be part of it all. It was magic, it was really cool. Whether it was with Kuwaitis or the many foreigners, no matter how hard you were working, you still could do more and you still got involved with more things. You could see the potential and just the way everybody worked together. I'm sure the American people felt like that after the Second World War . . . it was just something special.

"I have to say, I was also quite spoiled because I was an American. The respect given to Americans was absolutely phenomenal."

— **Katherine C. Baker**
General Manager, Amricani Cultural Center, Kuwait

Business office looted by marauding Iraqi soldiers. *Photo courtesy of Kuwait Ministry of Information.*

Celebrating soldiers and civilians hold Saudi and Kuwaiti flags aloft following the retreat of Iraqi forces from Kuwait. *Photo courtesy of NARA.*

Parliament and are active in a number of areas. With this added strength, the future looks bright for the country as Kuwaitis hope to leverage their many political, geographic, cultural, and economic advantages over the coming years.

While oil and other hydrocarbons account for about 95 percent of Kuwait's exports, the oil sector contributes only about 50 percent to Kuwait's gross domestic product. While that is certainly significant, it also demonstrates that Kuwait is becoming increasingly successful in diversifying its economy and using both national and personal wealth to expand into a variety of enterprises. The telecommunications industry, led by the giant Zain, is one example. Kuwaiti investors have also created and expanded into the low-cost airline market with Jazeera Airways.

FAMILY-FRIENDLY DESTINATIONS

Kuwait has a growing population that will require a steadily expanding economy to support the tens of thousands of new additions to the workforce. To accomplish this goal, Kuwait has embarked on a plan for becoming a powerful banking, service, and trading hub within the Gulf region and the greater Middle East. Kuwait is also seeking to expand its domestic tourist industry by offering greater entertainment opportunities, especially family-friendly destination resorts.

THE KUWAIT-U.S. ALLIANCE TODAY

To accomplish this economic expansion and broad-based development, Kuwait seeks to enhance its political and economic ties to western countries, particularly the United States. Kuwait hopes to offer mutually beneficial commercial, cultural, entertainment, and investment opportunities in these countries. Additionally, Kuwait has been an important military ally to the United States since the Gulf War and wants to continue that relationship.

Commercially, however, Kuwait is also looking east to the emerging economic giants of Asia. In true Kuwaiti fashion, the nation continues to be one of the most internationally engaged countries on earth. This strategic approach, in fact, will become increasingly essential in the years ahead. About 60 percent of Kuwaitis are under the age of 25. Kuwait has a population growth rate of about four percent—a sky-high number compared to the world average, close to 1.1 percent.

And these are dynamic youth—many studying abroad and learning to speak, read, and write in many languages other than their native Arabic. English is widely spoken in Kuwait and among Kuwaitis. Two leading Kuwaiti newspapers are published in English—*Arab Times* and *Kuwait Times*.

With its proverbial face to the future, Kuwait places strong emphasis on education. One hundred percent of Kuwaiti children attend primary and secondary public schools, paid for by the government. Private international schools in Kuwait are also popular and well-attended. Kuwait is a city-state where about 98 percent of the population resides in an urban setting. Kuwaitis are technologically savvy and engaged.

Today, when one stands on the seaside road facing Kuwait City, the most notable object is the skyline—a remarkable number of skyscrapers, new and under construction, fill the horizon from right to left. Kuwait City has changed since the war. It has grown up in more ways than one, and these towering, colorfully lit buildings give the city a dynamic look and the aura of optimism.

This can-do attitude is real—it can be felt in streets, in businesses, throughout the land. It can be seen in peoples' faces. This is a new Kuwait—ready, willing, and able to be a force for good in the world. ■

President Bush and His Highness the late Amir of Kuwait, Sheikh Jaber Al-Ahmad Al-Jaber Al-Sabah, wave to a supportive crowd gathered at the White House. *Photo courtesy of the George Bush Presidential Library and Museum.*

Chapter 9

ALLIANCE STRENGTHENED IN WAR, TEMPERED IN PEACE

Since the end of the Gulf War, the Kuwaiti government has made a consistent effort to work diplomatically to help Americans learn what happened during that war and how that victory has changed—and improved—both nations and their people. For example, in partnership with the Kuwait Ministry of Education, U.S. Ambassador Douglas Silliman visited a Kuwaiti girls school to speak about the two nations' friendship. The 82nd Airborne Five-Piece Brass Band performed alongside the school band, and afterward, Ambassador Silliman and several U.S. soldiers in uniform spoke to the girls gathered in the auditorium.

School visits such as this one, and numerous similar events and presentations, provide young Kuwaitis with an opportunity to hear the unique stories firsthand from the American veterans who served in Kuwait. What is more significant to America, perhaps, is that those stories are also important to the Kuwaiti government and people. Their leaders want the youth of Kuwait to know, to understand, and to remember.

Few Americans realize that Kuwait has a constitution containing protections similar to those found in the Constitution of the United States. Kuwait has created a system where individuals, regardless of color or creed, can work to improve their lives and lift themselves out of poverty. It has an elected parliament, chosen by the citizens. The parliament listens to its people—it considers and votes on a national budget, it regulates political policy.

All Americans, especially Gulf War veterans and their families, should be proud of their role in helping Kuwait become the free and prosperous nation it is today. As a people, Americans were willing to sacrifice much to accomplish what many thought impossible. Today, because of the service of honored U.S. veterans, the United States and the State of Kuwait are the closest of allies and friends. This relationship, strengthened in war, can be a force for good in a changing, challenging, and even dangerous world.

THE POWER OF TRADE AND COMMERCE

The United States and Kuwait have a keenly developed military relationship cemented in war that has remained firm for a quarter-century. Similarly, there is a close political relationship between the two nations, especially regarding the many challenging regional issues that face both Kuwait and the United States today. Kuwait has proven its effectiveness in helping combat terrorism at home and in the region.

In mediating regional disputes, Kuwaitis are skilled at working effectively behind the scenes, bringing disparate sides and factions together politically before they resort to military force. Kuwait and the United States also have a solid, expanding economic relationship, demonstrating how diplomacy and commerce often go hand in hand.

HONORING THOSE WHO SERVED

In the words of one of our soldiers prior to Operation Desert Storm: "They asked for our help. We are going to give them that help, free their country, go home, and carry on with life." It was a total team effort in the U.S. military and in our government. The magnificent will of President George H. W. Bush could be felt throughout the entire mission. The soldiers and their units were trained and ready. The military had undergone a renaissance of change dedicated to training and readiness and to "winning the first battle of the next war."

THE COMFORT OF FRIENDS

As America and Kuwait face an often uncertain future, it is comforting to know that these two nations can be more effective dealing with the inevitable challenges by facing them together as friends. The war taught those who were paying attention that in a dangerous and increasingly complicated world, and in an often unstable neighborhood, friends are not only desirable but essential. They can cover your back—they can save your life. ■

Seek Advice. Seek Information.

"It's important to remember that President Bush did not make a decision in the first couple of days. He thought about it, reflected on it; he got advice from others, which was his traditional pattern of decision-making. Seek advice. Seek information."

— **General Colin Powell,** *Chairman of the U.S. Joint Chiefs of Staff*

Lieutenant Colonel Gregory Maida (left) and Captain Donald Cook (center) review the cooperative changes made to Kuwaiti Naval Base (KNB) with Lieutenant General Fahad Al-Amir, Kuwaiti Armed Forces Chief of Staff. During his visit, Lieutenant General Al-Amir made a point of expressing his pride in the capability of both countries to work as a unified body of professionals at the KNB. *Photo courtesy of DOD.*

The Seabees of Naval Mobile Construction Battalions enjoy a tea with Warrant Officer Saleh Al-Anzi, manager of the Kuwait House for National Works Memorial Museum. *Photo courtesy of DOD.*

Letter to the American Gulf War Veteran

"On the 25th anniversary of liberation, this special occasion for all Kuwaitis, engraved inside every Kuwaiti's conscience, we must record with pride our gratitude and appreciation to our friends, the American people, for their sacrifice and dedication. This will be recorded by history, honoring this great nation, America, for its principles and actions in support of justice in the world.

"When we recall February 26, 1991, and the rebirth of a new Kuwait, we remember its moderate actions and its support to peaceful responses in the world, for development and aid programs, and for Kuwait's continual humanitarian message towards the world's poor and struggling. In support of Kuwait, at a critical moment, the American people decided to be true to their own principles and values to create and lead an unprecedented global coalition to stand by the side of the aggrieved State of Kuwait. America then stood until Kuwait was liberated and free once more.

"On behalf of Kuwait and its citizens, and on my behalf personally, I send an important and sincere message to all those who sacrificed and served in that honored war. We send you, America, a great 'thank you' from every Kuwaiti citizen, every man, woman, and child. The United States and her people will remain in our memory and our hearts. Our longtime friendship was built from the start on mutual respect for each other and respect of principles we have always shared. The Kuwaiti people remember that a century ago, the United States sent a humanitarian mission to provide medical services to Kuwait when there was none at that time.

"Kuwait knows that the American Constitution has always been interpreted and implemented by deeds and actions—by service—and not by words alone. The birth of a new Kuwait, which we celebrate, consolidated and focused our determination to stand always with the right cause in the world, to help other nations, and to always remember our true friends. The war to liberate Kuwait proved that friendship is built and nurtured from principles and not from selfish interests. Using the example of the Americans, following liberation, Kuwait returned to its tradition of extending a hand to the world through humanitarian actions and desires.

"That which links our two peoples will never be forgotten by Kuwaitis. It is engraved in our minds and hearts in a powerful appreciation to this great nation. At this time I wish to send a message to America's veteran heroes, a message of honored gratitude to them and to their families for their sacrifice to liberate Kuwait from a vicious aggressor.

"I also send a message to the martyrs' families and wish them peace and assure them that Kuwait will not forget their sacrifice and their generous service. Finally, I conclude with my special thanks from my own heart to our American friends, hoping that this important message will be translated into a deep, abiding relationship based upon respect and cooperation, an alliance as friends for the betterment of all humanity."

H.E. Sheikh Salman Al-Hamoud Al-Sabah
Kuwait Minister of Information
The State of Kuwait

Secretary of Defense Ash Carter presents a gift to Kuwait's Deputy Prime Minister and Minister of Defense Sheikh Khaled Al-Jarrah Al-Sabah while meeting with senior Kuwaiti officials in 2015. *Photo courtesy of DOD.*

Raising U.S. and Kuwaiti flags. *Photo courtesy of Kuwait Ministry of Information.*

Kuwaiti child shows gratitude for American friendship. *Photo courtesy of Kuwait Ministry of Information.*

A Balanced Friendship

"For decades, the United States imported a lot of our oil from Kuwait. As our domestic production has gone up, what we have imported from Kuwait is beginning to go down, but our trade balance has not changed because Kuwaitis like American products and American brands.

"When you come here, not only can you eat in a McDonald's or a KFC, but you can eat at The Cheesecake Factory, you can shop at Dean & DeLuca, you can go to West Elm or many other American outlets, because Kuwaitis have developed a cultural affinity for the United States. That makes us politically *and* economically close.

"One of our major goals is to help rebuild a new basis for another 25 years of a powerful relationship. I think that basis is going to be education. There are about 10,000 Kuwaiti students in the United States right now. Although that may not seem like a big number in absolute terms, it represents about 10 percent of graduating Kuwaiti high school seniors. It is very significant to the education and culture of Kuwait.

"I think it is going to be through the process of Kuwaitis growing up, becoming familiar with the American way of doing things, learning how to speak English better than they did from just book-learned English. Those are the things that are going to develop the ties that will take us through the next generation of our relationship.

"Again, we are always looking back at the past to appreciate and honor the people who serve and who suffered and who gave the ultimate sacrifice to liberate their country, to protect international law, to help liberate Kuwait. We also have a responsibility to look forward and find out how we can build a new relationship, how the United States and Kuwait can continue this very close relationship into the future."

— **Ambassador Douglas Silliman**
   U.S. Ambassador to Kuwait (2014-Present)

Kuwaiti Bonds Forged by War

"The impact of that occupation on Kuwait and on Kuwaitis a quarter of a century later is still, I think, fairly intense. Their experience is something an American, mercifully, can never understand. As several Kuwaitis put it to me, 'We went to bed Kuwaiti, and we woke up Iraqi. Our country disappeared overnight.'

"In addition to the trauma of the violence of having friends and relatives captured and killed, the psychological nightmare of losing your country is still deeply felt among Kuwaitis who are old enough to remember the invasion. Just as it still exists with my friends and colleagues who were in the American Embassy. That just won't go away. These are life-changing, life-shaping events. It is a fraternity and sorority of those Americans and Kuwaitis who went through occupation and liberation together. It's one of the strongest bonds I've ever seen."

— **Ambassador Ryan Crocker,** *U.S. Ambassador to Kuwait (1994-97)*

Kuwaiti Friendship

"The Kuwaitis gave us a gorgeous medal. We all wore it very proudly, and were thrilled to get our copy of the medal provided to everyone who fought to liberate Kuwait.

"I have certainly met a lot of Kuwaitis since then, and they all know exactly what the Left Hook was. They all are very appreciative of us helping liberate their country. They are thrilled to be allies, and they are thrilled to be allies from long before Desert Storm. I think we'll be allies and friends for an awfully long time."

— **Major General (ret) John Macdonald**
Squadron Operations Officer,
2nd Armored Cavalry Regiment, Desert Storm

American Pride

"I think it had a big impact on the psyche of the nation because I think at the end of Desert Storm, America really felt good about herself. We had a very positive president. We had military leaders like Colin Powell who essentially became iconic figures with enormous respect. We had the whole world that was saying, 'Good job.' I think the American people and the military were very proud, and it showed in the things we experienced after Desert Storm."

— **General (ret) Ronald Griffith**
Commander, 1st Armored Division, Desert Storm

President George H. W. Bush receives
a salute from General Schwarzkopf.
Photo courtesy of NARA.

Fraternity of Service

"This is not a story about me, a young kid from New England who ended up in command of an Aegis cruiser in the middle of a fire fight. No, it's the story of the hundreds of young men who spent hours, days, just making it all work.

"I had the most remarkable crew, the most remarkable executive officer, the best board room, and finest chief's mess. It was because of them that we were successful. That feeling of brotherhood, fraternity, cooperation—that's the thing I miss most about my naval service. There was this automatic feeling that we were all in it together, that there was no recrimination. No 'Well, you could have done it a different way.' It was, 'Yes, Sir. We will make this happen. We will get it done.'

"They kept on going. They went way beyond anybody's expectations or even ability to conceive what might be happening. They kept that flight deck rolling 24 hours a day as the only Shell station, if you will, in that part of the world for helicopters. They provided close air control 24 hours a day, seven days a week, week after week. They did it supremely well because of their level of professionalism. That extended down to the mess groups in the galley who kept hot food flowing for four meals a day because we were on 12-hour-off watch cycle.

"That was my ship, and that feeling was mirrored on many other ships and carriers throughout the force. It was one of those things where it was magic moments in time when we had ships from other countries, from the U.K., from Holland, from Canada, from Austrailia, all working together. I could go on, but you get the idea that it was a special time for us. It was a great privilege to be part of that at that point in our lives where we were ready. We had the right equipment, we had the right mission. We knew what we needed to do to accomplish it.

"That, I think, is one of the high points of my life. I think I'll always remember the men and women. I still am in touch with many of them. I get emails and 'Happy Fourth of July' messages from many. It is, I think, a profound sense of gratitude that we were able to do what we did and to always remember those who we lost."

— **Rear Admiral (ret) Tom Marfiak**
   Commander, Gulf Anti-Air Warfare, Desert Storm

Lessons of Diplomacy

"I think it is a lesson that Kuwait has learned very well [the power of friends and allies]. The current Amir of Kuwait, His Highness Sheikh Sabah Al-Ahmad Al-Jaber Al-Sabah, was the foreign minister at the time of the invasion and helped orchestrate this diplomatic triumph of building a very large coalition of both military and diplomatic forces. As he continued on as foreign minister and certainly as Amir today, Kuwait has tried very hard to build a broad and deep range of international relationships. Diplomacy for Kuwait is very important."

— **Ambassador Douglas Silliman**
   U.S. Ambassador to Kuwait (2014 - Present)

President Bush visits with troops.
Photo courtesy of the George Bush Presidential Library and Museum.

Kuwaiti officials discuss plans to extinguish burning wells. *Photo courtesy of Kuwait Ministry of Information.*

Kuwait Towers, Kuwait City. *Photo courtesy of Richard Bartz. Used under the Creative Commons license.*

Chapter 10

GIVING BACK—AN ENDURING LEGACY

Saddam's failure early on to decapitate Kuwait's leadership marked the beginning of his ultimate failure to steal and hold the nation of Kuwait. In fact, Saddam tried on many fronts—including meeting with Joseph Wilson, American senior representative in Baghdad during the occupation. At that time, Saddam offered to provide America with oil at "one-third the market price for life" if the United States would allow him to keep Kuwait. Such was the depravity and corruption of this tyrant.

OUR STRUGGLE WAS NEVER WITH THE IRAQI PEOPLE

Before the Gulf War, Kuwait consistently made the case that its struggle was never with the Iraqi people, but with Saddam and his aggressive policies. Since the war, Kuwait has once again extended a brotherly hand of friendship to Iraq, providing assistance to and supporting the struggling government with its various geopolitical, economic, ethnic, and sectarian challenges.

Today, Kuwaiti officials meet regularly with the Iraqis, coordinating a number of assistance and exchange programs, helping where they can. In 2015, Kuwait provided aid to leading Kurdish groups to support and protect Kurdish civilians fleeing war-torn regions.

Of course, such aid is not entirely altruistic. When neighbors and friends are threatened, the wise understand they have a stake in the outcome and prudently get involved. Kuwait's leaders make it a policy to not ignore a festering problem. Since the war, Kuwait has engaged on all necessary political levels, trying to keep small issues from becoming big ones.

A LEGACY OF GIVING BACK

Even before the war, Kuwait had quietly built a legacy of helping those in need, much like the United States. Many of the world's poorest, struggling nations in Africa and Asia received Kuwait's help from a variety of development funds and programs the country had established or to which it contributed. From Sri Lanka to the Maldives, from Morocco to Syria, Kuwait has led the way in providing critical and timely assistance, and in raising awareness through special humanitarian conferences hosted in Kuwait City on multiple occasions since the 1960s.

Most recently, due to the extreme needs of millions of refugees from the Syrian and Iraqi crises, Kuwait has actually stepped up its efforts, hosting support and assistance conferences in both 2014 and 2015, funneling hundreds of millions of its own dollars to aid these worthy projects.

EVERY SOLDIER A DIPLOMAT

One of the little-recognized benefits of the Gulf War was the way the American and Kuwaiti peoples came together as friends and allies. When hundreds of thousands of American veterans returned home in 1991, they became, in effect, diplomats for Kuwait, helping the American people learn of their appreciative friends in Kuwait, a people for whom America had sacrificed much to liberate.

A quarter-century has passed since the war. The Kuwaitis again want to thank America and her veterans for their willingness to restore Kuwaiti homes, lands, and lives. Many still find it hard to believe that anyone would be willing to travel halfway around the world and risk life and limb to come to their rescue. Yet Kuwaitis also realize that this is the legacy the United States created—this is what America has done in many lands and wars and for countless peoples since the country's founding two centuries ago.

Notwithstanding the ease of "friending" on modern social media, surely it is impossible to truly befriend someone on an intimate level without personal, human contact. Human nature has consistently proved that individual sacrifice and service on behalf of another nearly always endears those who are doing the sacrificing, bonding them forever to those they've protected and saved.

Most American Soldiers, Sailors, Airmen, Marines, and Coast Guardsmen returned home feeling good about what they had done to restore Kuwait as a free nation. In fact, they had sacrificed greatly to accomplish this and had received heartfelt gratitude from those they had rescued, a gratitude still felt strongly today.

KUWAIT, THE UNITED STATES, AND A CHANGING WORLD

Nothing is more certain in the world than change. But the challenge for Kuwait and the United States was—and still is—dealing with the dangers that radical change often brings. The Coalition response in 1991, backed by the United Nations, went beyond supporting Kuwait in its just claim against Saddam's larceny. That response, those actions, became in the greater global realm a statement to tyrants and belligerents everywhere.

The Coalition confronted Saddam not only to restore Kuwait's sovereignty but also as a warning to despots everywhere. What was unique about what both the United States and Kuwait brought to the U.N. coalition was the message of why this wrong could not stand. To accomplish such a worthy task, in the end, was dependent upon legitimate and capable leadership—leaders who refused to be cowed by a dictator.

Following liberation, the State of Kuwait determined not only to rebuild its nation but to move effectively toward greater political liberalization and a broad-based democratization. The Kuwaiti Parliament was restored, and not just as a "façade" body as we see in so many

Our Fight Is with Saddam

"We've always said that our fight was with Saddam and his regime alone. It was never with the Iraqi people. We've lived side-by-side with the Iraqis for centuries, and we will live with them for eternity. It was always with Saddam. Saddam was a brutal man. Saddam was a man who ruled his country harshly, who killed more Iraqis than any other people or nationalities, even to the last day of his regime. He was a very unpredictable, brutal criminal."

— **Sheikh Salem Al-Sabah**
Kuwaiti Ambassador to the United States

Giving Back

"Our donations and philanthropic work did not start with the invasion of Kuwait—we were always involved. We donate a percentage of our income every year to needy countries, and we have a special fund called the 'Kuwait Fund.' The Fund [director] goes around the world, looking at projects and countries, and the Kuwaiti Fund helps implement those projects.

"Giving has always been part of our policy, part of our diplomacy. In September 2014, Ban Ki-moon, the U.N. secretary-general, designated the Amir of Kuwait, Sheikh Sabah, as a humanitarian leader because of the work that Kuwait does. Now we are in the midst of the Syrian crisis. Kuwait has hosted three conferences for Syria that have grossed almost $8 billion. Kuwait alone has contributed $1.3 billion.

"We never forget that we are blessed with wealth. We must always make certain to share that wealth. Giving to other needy countries was not begun by our liberation. Giving is part of our DNA."

— **Sheikh Salem Al-Sabah**
Kuwaiti Ambassador to the United States

Kuwait: A History of Giving

"What I understand from having lived in Kuwait for over 30 years is that the history of Kuwait and its generosity goes back a long way. Kuwait has had such a positive impact as a small country. What they have done and continue to do is to share their good fortune they have gotten [through] oil. They have always shared with those in need, and they continue to do so."

— **Katherine C. Baker**
General Manager, Amricani Cultural Center, Kuwait

Aerial view of martyrs Park in Kuwait City. *Photo courtesy of Kuwait Ministry of Information.*

One of many new public sites and commercial developments built in post-war Kuwait. *Photo courtesy of Kuwait Ministry of Information.*

A crowd of well-wishers at Naval Air Station Oceana, Virginia, welcome home LT Jeffrey Zaun, LT Lawrence Slade, and LT Robert Wetzel during a ceremony in their honor. The three pilots were shot down over Iraq and held prisoner until they were released on March 4, 1991. *Photo courtesy of NARA.*

Welcome home for POWs of the Gulf War. *Photo courtesy of NARA.*

A sailor assigned to USS *Fort McHenry* (LSD 43) is reunited with his parents on the pier, following its deployment to the Arabian Gulf for Operation Desert Shield and Operation Desert Storm. *Photo courtesy of NARA.*

dictatorships today, but as a genuine, functioning, operating parliament.

In 2005, Kuwaiti women received the right to vote. Today, Kuwaiti women arguably have greater rights than any other women in the Gulf region. Women serve in the parliament, they serve in the executive cabinet, they are CEOs and senior officers in powerful companies, and they work in all areas of government and business. They play a vital role in Kuwaiti life and contribute much to the improvement and progress of the nation.

In fact, it is likely that much of this liberalization grew directly out of victory and liberation—women also wanted to contribute to the rebuilding and expansion of post-war Kuwait. After all, women had fought, sacrificed, and died during occupation, serving in the resistance and in building global political awareness of Kuwait's struggle.

WHERE MUCH IS GIVEN, MUCH IS EXPECTED

A coalition from many nations—led by the most powerful and capable nation on earth—arose to face wickedness and oppose a tyrant. These volunteers came *en masse*, at great expense and risk, from safe homes and loved ones a world away. But they were not plunderers. They came to do a tough job and then return home, with nothing but the thanks and admiration of those they had served. In this they were one of the most unusual armies ever assembled. This coalition of allies understood who they were and why they were there. They created one special moment in time when the world came together behind capable

The Generosity of Kuwait

"Kuwait has been particularly generous as a humanitarian donor. Very interestingly, and maybe ironically, they have also provided significant political and economic support to the government of Iraq.

"I was in Baghdad in 2012 when the Iraqis hosted the Arab League Summit. Most of the leaders of the Arab world didn't want to come to Baghdad, for they were worried about the security threat and that it was not convenient for them. But His Highness the Amir of Kuwait, Sheikh Sabah, was one leader who really made an impression in Iraq by coming personally to attend the summit.

"Following that, he provided a lot of political and financial support to the Iraqi government, up to and including delaying for two years the final reparations payment that Iraq owes Kuwait. In addition to that, this year he pledged $200 million in humanitarian assistance, which is now being delivered by the Kuwaiti Red Crescent and representatives of the Kuwaiti Foreign Ministry in parts of Iraq today.

"The generosity of Kuwait is not only for sub-Saharan Africa. They have built schools in poor countries of Asia and have also helped to develop the business infrastructure in needy places in southern Europe where they have helped restore inner cities. Kuwait actually goes so far as to help their one-time foe Iraq rebuild their nation and achieve political stability. From conversations I've had with the Amir, he's very committed to continuing the support for Iraq."

— **Ambassador Douglas Silliman**, *U.S. Ambassador to Kuwait (2014-Present)*

leaders determined to right a wrong and to restore a worthy nation and people.

Nearly all human beings understand that where much is given, much is expected. The members of the Coalition lived by that creed. In fact, the United States and the State of Kuwait had always embodied it. In the end, that would be their legacy: courage, selfless service, and sacrifice that would inspire the free world and put fear into the hearts of tyrants everywhere. Such was the legacy and gift of the heroes of Desert Storm. These are the men and women we honor today. ■

A view of Iraqi armored personnel carriers, tanks and trucks destroyed in a Coalition attack along a road in the Euphrates River Valley during Operation Desert Storm. *Photo courtesy of Defense Media Network.*

Unofficial Ambassadors

"I think that what Kuwait gained, certainly beyond being liberated and restored to their original lands, was that they were so kind to our soldiers. Even though some soldiers may not have had a chance to get into Kuwait City, we felt the warmth and the gratitude from Kuwaitis for what we had done.

"I think what happened was that all those American veterans became ambassadors back in the United States for Kuwait, and supporters for the reason we went. You see that quite often. The soldier that goes in has to do a job. It's a tough job. I know this is difficult for 99 percent of Americans to understand. But when our veterans came back from Kuwait, they were very positive. They were unofficial ambassadors for Kuwait."

— **Lieutenant General (ret) Dan Petrosky**
Commander, Aviation Brigade, 1st Armored Division, Desert Storm

Honoring Those Who Did Not Return

"I feel privileged to still be here to pay great honor and respect to all those who served in VII Corps, and also to pay everlasting honor and respect to those who, in Lincoln's words, did not return, who gave that last full measure of devotion. To that end, we formed a VII Corps Desert Storm Veterans Association, where each year we hold a reunion of camaraderie, and we also have a memorial service where we read each name of those—British and American— who did not return."

— **General (ret) Fred Franks**
Commander, VII Corps, Desert Storm

Kuwaiti citizens attend to a damaged mosaic. Photo courtesy of Kuwait Ministry of Information.

A CH-53E Super Stallion helicopter from Helicopter Combat Support Squadron 1 (HC-1) stands on the deck of an amphibious assault ship in the Arabian Gulf. *Photo courtesy of NARA.*

Stability Through Victory

"The significance of the liberation of Kuwait at the time was pretty large. First of all, it was a nonbelligerent country that had unfairly and in a devastating fashion been attacked. The fact that the allied victory in Kuwait was successful showed that there are still forces of good in the world that would not let this happen. The other significance is the national interest of not only the United States but other countries around the globe, and especially the region, which needed the very stability that a sound victory provided. Only through victory over tyranny can modern, peaceful daily life, both individual life and national life, continue in the world."

— **Lieutenant General (ret) Roger Thompson**
Commander, 34th Transportation Group Europe, Desert Storm

Partners Into Allies

"Prior to the invasion, we were friends with America, but the invasion created a special relationship. It was a fork in the road, a turning point in our relationship with the United States. It turned us from friends and partners into allies, very strong allies. In 2004, President George Bush designated Kuwait as a major non-NATO ally, a designation of only 15 or 16 countries around the world. That shows how much our relationship has grown. Today we consider ourselves strategic allies with the United States. Prior to 1990, we were friends and partners, but post-1991, we became strategic allies. It was a huge leap forward in our bilateral relationship.

"Kuwait will always be grateful to the United States. You gave us back our nation. You gave us back our homeland. Who would do that, honestly? But you did. The American people did it, and that's why you are who you are today in the world, because you stand for righteousness and justice.

"Again, I want to emphasize we are where we are today in our Kuwaiti American relationship because of what happened 25 years ago. The relationship has grown exponentially ever since. God willing, it will keep growing."

— **Sheikh Salem Al-Sabah**
Kuwaiti Ambassador to the United States

PRESIDENT GEORGE H. W. BUSH
STATE OF THE UNION
Excerpts
March 6, 1991

Members of Congress, five short weeks ago I came to this House to speak to you about the state of the Union. We met then in time of war. Tonight, we meet in a world blessed by the promise of peace.

From the moment Operation Desert Storm commenced on January 16th until the time the guns fell silent at midnight one week ago, this nation has watched its sons and daughters with pride, watched over them with prayer. As Commander in Chief, I can report to you our armed forces fought with honor and valor. And as President, I can report to the nation aggression is defeated. The war is over.

This is a victory for every country in the coalition, for the United Nations. A victory for unprecedented international cooperation and diplomacy, so well led by our Secretary of State, James Baker. It is a victory for the rule of law and for what is right.

Desert Storm's success belongs to the team that so ably leads our Armed Forces: our Secretary of Defense and our Chairman of the Joint Chiefs, Dick Cheney and Colin Powell... This military victory also belongs to the one the British call the "Man of the Match"—the tower of calm at the eye of Desert Storm—General Norman Schwarzkopf.

And recognizing this was a coalition effort, let us not forget Saudi General Khalid bin Sultan, Britain's General de la Billiere, or General Michel Roquejeoffre of France, and all the others whose leadership played such a vital role. And most importantly, most importantly of all, all those who served in the field.

I thank the members of this Congress—support here for our troops in battle was overwhelming. And above all, I thank those whose unfailing love and support sustained our courageous men and women: I thank the American people.

Tonight, I come to this House to speak about the world—the world after war. The recent challenge could not have been clearer. Saddam Hussein was the villain; Kuwait, the victim. To the aid of this small country came nations from North America and Europe, from Asia and South America, from Africa and the Arab world, all united against aggression. Our uncommon coalition must now work in common purpose: to forge a future that should never again be held hostage to the darker side of human nature.

Tonight in Iraq, Saddam walks amidst ruin. His war machine is crushed. His ability to threaten mass destruction is itself destroyed. His people have been lied to, denied the truth. And when his defeated legions come home, all Iraqis will see and feel the havoc he has wrought. And this I promise you: for all that Saddam has done to his own people, to the Kuwaitis, and to the entire world, Saddam and those around him are accountable.

All of us grieve for the victims of war, for the people of Kuwait and the suffering that scars the soul of that proud nation. We grieve for all our fallen soldiers and their families, for all the innocents caught up in this conflict. And, yes, we grieve for the people of Iraq, a people who have never been our enemy. My hope is that one day we will once again welcome them as friends into the community of nations. Our commitment to peace in the Middle East does not end with the liberation of Kuwait. So, tonight let me outline four key challenges to be met.

First, we must work together to create shared security arrangements in the region. Our friends and allies in the Middle East recognize that they will bear the bulk of the responsibility for regional security. But we want them to know that just as we stood with them to repel aggression, so now America stands ready to work with them to secure the peace... Let it be clear: Our vital national interests depend on a stable and secure Gulf.

Second, we must act to control the proliferation of weapons of mass destruction and the missiles used to deliver them. It would be tragic if the nations of the Middle East and Arabian Gulf were now, in the wake of war, to embark on a new arms race...

And third, we must work to create new opportunities for peace and stability in the Middle East. On the night I announced Operation Desert Storm, I expressed my hope that out of the horrors of war might come new momentum for peace... There can be no substitute for diplomacy.

Fourth, we must foster economic development for the sake of peace and progress. The Arabian Gulf and Middle East form a region rich in natural resources with a wealth of untapped human potential. Resources once squandered on military might must be redirected to more peaceful ends... Now, the challenge is to reach higher, to foster economic freedom and prosperity for all the people of the region.

By meeting these four challenges we can build a framework for peace. I've asked Secretary of State Baker to go to the Middle East to begin the process. He will go to listen, to probe, to offer suggestions—to advance the search for peace and stability... To all the challenges that confront this region of the world there is no single solution, no solely American answer. But we can make a difference. America will work tirelessly as a catalyst for positive change...

The consequences of the conflict in the Gulf reach far beyond the confines of the Middle East... For the sake of our principles, for the sake of the Kuwaiti people, we stood our ground. Because the world would not look the other way, Ambassador Al-Sabah, tonight Kuwait is free. And we're very happy about that...

When I spoke in this House about the state of our Union, I asked all of you: If we can selflessly confront evil for the sake of good in a land so far away, then surely we can make this land all that it should be. In the time since then, the brave men and women of Desert Storm accomplished more than even they may realize. They set out to confront an enemy abroad, and in the process, they transformed a nation at home. Think of the way they went about their mission—with confidence and quiet pride. Think about

Thanksgiving with the troops during Desert Shield.
Photo courtesy of the George Bush Presidential Library and Museum.

their sense of duty, about all they taught us about our values, about ourselves...

The America we saw in Desert Storm was first-class talent. And they did it using America's state-of-the-art technology. We saw the excellence embodied in the Patriot missile and the patriots who made it work. And we saw soldiers who know about honor and bravery and duty and country and the world-shaking power of these simple words. There is something noble and majestic about the pride, about the patriotism that we feel tonight.

So, to everyone here and everyone watching at home, think about the men and women of Desert Storm. Let us honor them with our gratitude. Let us comfort the families of the fallen and remember each precious life lost.

Let us learn from them as well. Let us honor those who have served us by serving others. Let us honor them as individuals—men and women of every race, all creeds and colors—by setting the face of this nation against discrimination, bigotry, and hate. Eliminate them.

I'm sure that many of you saw on the television the unforgettable scene of four terrified Iraqi soldiers surrendering. They emerged from their bunker broken, tears streaming from their eyes, fearing the worst. And then there was an American soldier. Remember what he said? He said: "It's okay. You're all right now. You're all right now." That scene says a lot about America, a lot about who we are. Americans are a caring people. We are a good people, a generous people. Let us always be caring and good and generous in all we do.

Soon, very soon, our troops will begin the march we've all been waiting for—their march home. And I have directed Secretary Cheney to begin the immediate return of American combat units from the Gulf. Less than two hours from now, the first planeload of American soldiers will lift off from Saudi Arabia, headed for the U.S.A. That plane will carry the men and women of the 24th Mechanized Infantry Division bound for Fort Stewart, Georgia. This is just the beginning of a steady flow of American troops coming home. Let their return remind us that all those who have gone before are linked with us in the long line of freedom's march.

In a very real sense, this victory belongs to them—to the privates and the pilots, to the sergeants and the supply officers, to the men and women in the machines and the men and women who made them work. It belongs to the regulars, to the reserves, to the National Guard. This victory belongs to the finest fighting force this nation has ever known in its history.

We went halfway around the world to do what is moral and just and right. We fought hard and, with others, we won the war. We lifted the yoke of aggression and tyranny from a small country that many Americans had never even heard of, and we ask nothing in return.

We're coming home now—proud, confident, heads high. There is much that we must do, at home and abroad. And we will do it. We are Americans.

May God bless this great nation, the United States of America. Thank you all very, very much. ■

President George H. W. Bush speaks by phone with British Prime Minister John Major during a meeting with Secretary Dick Cheney, General Colin Powell (speaks by phone with General Norman Schwarzkopf), National Security Advisor Brent Scowcroft, Governor John Sununu, and advisor Robert Gates in the Oval Office, February 27, 1991. *Photo courtesy of the George Bush Presidential Library and Museum.*

General Colin Powell, Chairman of the U.S. Joint Chiefs of Staff, briefs the press on the U.S. military response to the Iraqi invasion of Kuwait. *Photo courtesy of NARA.*

GENERAL COLIN POWELL
CHAIRMAN OF THE JOINT CHIEFS OF STAFF
Excerpts

June 27, 1991 — Stuttgart, Germany

"The battle was won not only because of your prowess in the desert, but because your buddies back here were supporting all of you fighting in Operation Desert Storm.

"It was a magnificent joint team effort—Army, Navy, Air Force, Marine Corps, Coast Guard, Civilians, EUCOM, CENTCOM, and all the other specified and unified commands of the United States Armed Forces, and of our allies working together. Working together for one singular reason, so that on the battlefield, at the point of decision, we would win. And we did win!

"The threat that Saddam Hussein posed to the region ten months ago is gone. Those nations can now feel secure. You have raised the levels of warfare to new heights. You fought a war of complexity and integration no one has ever seen before. You were at the very top of the profession of arms, and we had lots of critics who said that we would not be able to do it. We had critics who said that our equipment wouldn't work. We had critics who said that the 'all-volunteer force,' this magnificent all-volunteer force, was not up to the challenge. We had critics who said that we had people in command who were managers and not leaders, managers who were not warriors. They said our training was inadequate; they said we did not know how to do complex operations 8,000 miles away from home. All those critics and all those 'experts' are now looking for a new line of work. Because you showed we could do it.

"But wars are never without losses. Some of our buddies were lost. We grieve for them. We grieve for their families. We will never, never forget their sacrifice.

"And there is one group of individuals who served more valiantly than anyone else—your families. Your families who also answered the call of duty by waiting anxiously, by taking care of each other, by supporting you and by being there when you came home. We will never forget the contributions of your families.

"You have made America proud and you have made America feel good about herself again! You have made America realize that there is nothing we can't do if we put our hearts to it, if we put our minds to it, and if we put our muscles to the task before us.

"As your chairman, I am enormously proud of you. Enjoy the adulation you now receive. Thank you all and God bless you." ■

Kuwait water towers. *Photo licensed from iStock.*

OUR DISTINGUISHED SPONSORS

We extend our warmest regards and deepest, heartfelt gratitude to the following individuals and their companies and organizations for their vision and financial support of this worthy project to honor the American and Kuwaiti Veterans of the Gulf War, also known as Operation Desert Storm.

This commemorative book and companion feature documentary are but small gifts offered to our honored Veterans to help record and remember their service and sacrifice, and to help future generations understand what has been accomplished on their behalf and at a high price.

Thank you to the following for making this possible:

The State of Kuwait

Fouad Alghanim and Sons Group
Mr. Fouad M. T. Alghanim, Chairman

Kuwait Banking Association
Dr. Hamad A. Al-Hasawi, Secretary General

Morad Yusuf Behbehani Group
Mr. Ali Morad Behbehani, President

Mr. Mohammad Shahid Islam
Partner, MD/CEO
Marafie Kuwaitia Group of Companies

Raytheon Company
Gary Menke, President
Raytheon International Kuwait

25TH ANNIVERSARY
THE
LIBERATION
OF
KUWAIT
HONORING THE VETERANS
OF DESERT STORM

A Remember My Service Publication

Special Thanks to:

The United States Embassy, Kuwait
The Martyrs Bureau, State of Kuwait
Ministry of Foreign Affairs, State of Kuwait
Ministry of Defense, State of Kuwait
Ministry of Information, State of Kuwait
Kuwait News Agency (KUNA)
Naval Historical Foundation
Association of the U.S. Army
George Bush Presidential Library and Museum
U.S. National Archives and Records Administration

PUBLISHING CREDITS

Author: **Rick Robison**

Publisher: **John Lund**

Executive Editor: **Sharlene Hawkes**

Advising Editor: **GEN (ret) Fred Franks**

Production Director: **Daryl Guiver**

Art Director: **Darren Nelson**

Senior Editor: **Elayne Wells Harmer**

Editor: **Kellene Ricks Adams**

Consultants: **MG (ret) John Macdonald**
Frank Nader
COL (ret) Rick Kiernan
MG (ret) Pat Condon

Interview Director: **Brandon Young**

Production Assistant: **Ike Hall**

Research Assistants: **Renee Casati**
Peggy Mitchell
Rebecca Thomas
Madison Harmer

Photo Researcher: **Gina McNeely**